Paper C02

FUNDAMENTALS OF FINANCIAL ACCOUNTING

CIMA EXAM PRACTICE KIT

CIMA
PUBLISHING

KAPLAN
PUBLISHING

Published by: Kaplan Publishing UK

Unit 2 The Business Centre, Molly Millars Lane, Wokingham, Berkshire RG41 2QZ

Acknowledgements

The CIMA Publishing trade mark is reproduced with kind permission of CIMA.

We are also grateful to CIMA for permission to reproduce past examination questions. The answers to CIMA Exams have been prepared by Kaplan Publishing, except in the case of the CIMA November 2010 and subsequent CIMA Exam answers where the official CIMA answers have been reproduced.

British Library Cataloguing in Publication Data

A catalogue record for this book is available from the British Library

ISBN: 978-0-85732-963-9

Printed and bound in Great Britain.

CONTENTS

INDEX TO QUESTIONS AND ANSWERS

PRACTICE QUESTIONS

OBJECTIVE TEST QUESTIONS

SYLLABUS GUIDANCE, LEARNING OBJECTIVES AND VERBS

A THE CERTIFICATE IN BUSINESS ACCOUNTING

The Certificate introduces you to management accounting and gives you the basics of accounting and business. There are five subject areas, which are all tested by computer-based assessment (CBA). The five papers are:

- Fundamentals of Management Accounting
- Fundamentals of Financial Accounting
- Fundamentals of Business Mathematics
- Fundamentals of Business Economics
- Fundamentals of Ethics, Corporate Governance and Business Law

The Certificate is both a qualification in its own right and an entry route to the next stage in CIMA's examination structure.

The examination structure after the Certificate comprises:

- Managerial Level
- Strategic Level
- Test of Professional Competence (an exam based on a case study).

This examination structure includes more advanced papers in Financial Accounting. It is therefore very important that you work hard at Fundamentals of Financial Accounting, not only because it is part of the Certificate, but also as a platform for more advanced studies. It is thus an important step in becoming a qualified member of the Chartered Institute of Management Accountants.

B AIMS OF THE SYLLABUS

The aims of the syllabus are

- to provide for the Institute, together with the practical experience requirements, an adequate basis for assuring society that those admitted to membership are competent to act as management accountants for entities, whether in manufacturing, commercial or service organisations, in the public or private sectors of the economy;
- to enable the Institute to examine whether prospective members have an adequate knowledge, understanding and mastery of the stated body of knowledge and skills;
- to complement the Institute's practical experience and skills development requirements.

C STUDY WEIGHTINGS

A percentage weighting is shown against each topic in the syllabus. This is intended as a guide to the proportion of study time each topic requires.

All topics in the syllabus must be studied, since any single examination question may examine more than one topic, or carry a higher proportion of marks than the percentage study time suggested.

The weightings do not specify the number of marks that will be allocated to topics in the examination.

D LEARNING OUTCOMES

Each topic within the syllabus contains a list of learning outcomes, which should be read in conjunction with the knowledge content for the syllabus. A learning outcome has two main purposes:

1   to define the skill or ability that a well-prepared candidate should be able to exhibit in the examination;

2   to demonstrate the approach likely to be taken by examiners in examination questions.

The learning outcomes are part of a hierarchy of learning objectives. The verbs used at the beginning of each learning outcome relate to a specific learning objective, e.g. Evaluate alternative approaches to budgeting.

The verb 'evaluate' indicates a high-level learning objective. As learning objectives are hierarchical, it is expected that at this level students will have knowledge of different budgeting systems and methodologies and be able to apply them.

A list of the learning objectives and the verbs that appear in the syllabus learning outcomes and examinations follows.

Learning objectives	Verbs used	Definition
1 Knowledge		
What you are expected to know	List	Make a list of
	State	Express, fully or clearly, the details of/facts of
	Define	Give the exact meaning of
2 Comprehension		
What you are expected to understand	Describe	Communicate the key features of
	Distinguish	Highlight the differences between
	Explain	Make clear or intelligible/State the meaning of
	Identify	Recognise, establish or select after consideration
	Illustrate	Use an example to describe or explain something

3	**Application**		
	How you are expected to apply your knowledge	Apply	To put to practical use
		Calculate/compute	To ascertain or reckon mathematically
		Demonstrate	To prove with certainty or to exhibit by practical means
		Prepare	To make or get ready for use
		Reconcile	To make or prove consistent/compatible
		Solve	Find an answer to
		Tabulate	Arrange in a table
4	**Analysis**		
	How you are expected to analyse the detail of what you have learned	Analyse	Examine in detail the structure of
		Categorise	Place into a defined class or division
		Compare and contrast	Show the similarities and/or differences between
		Construct	To build up or compile
		Discuss	To examine in detail by argument
		Interpret	To translate into intelligible or familiar terms
		Produce	To create or bring into existence
5	**Evaluation**	**Evaluation**	
	How you are expected to use your learning to evaluate, make decisions or recommendations	Advise	To counsel, inform or notify
		Evaluate	To appraise or assess the value of
		Recommend	To advise on a course of action

E COMPUTER-BASED ASSESSMENT

CIMA has introduced computer-based assessment (CBA) for all subjects at Certificate level. CIMA uses objective test questions in the computer-based assessment. The most common types are:

- multiple choice, where you have to choose the correct answer from a list of four possible answers. This could either be numbers or text.

- multiple choice with more choices and answers – for example, choosing two correct answers from a list of eight possible answers. This could either be numbers or text.

- single numeric entry, where you give your numeric answer e.g. profit is 10000

- multiple entry, where you give several numeric answers e.g. the charge for electricity is 2000 and the accrual is 200

- true/false questions, where you state whether a statement is true or false e.g. external auditors report to the directors is FALSE.

- matching pairs of text e.g. the convention 'prudence' would be matched with the statement' inventories revalued at the lower of cost and net realisable value'.

- other types could be matching text with graphs and labelling graphs/diagrams.

In this Exam Practice Kit we have used these types of questions.

Some further guidance from CIMA on number entry questions is as follows:

- For number entry questions, you do not need to include currency symbols or other characters or symbols such as the percentage sign, as these will have been completed for you. You may use the decimal point but must not use any other characters when entering an answer (except numbers) so, for example, $10,500.80 would be input as 10500.80

- When expressing a decimal, for example a probability or correlation coefficient, you should include the leading zero (i.e. you should input 0.5 not .5)

- Negative numbers should be input using the minus sign, for example −1000

- You will receive an error message if you try to enter a character or symbol that is not permitted (for example a '£' or '%' sign)

- A small range of answers will normally be accepted, taking into account sensible rounding

Guidance re CIMA online calculator:

As part of the CIMA Certificate level computer based assessment software, candidates are now provided with a calculator. This calculator is onscreen and is available for the duration of the assessment. The calculator is available in each of the five Certificate level assessments and is accessed by clicking the calculator button in the top left hand corner of the screen at any time during the assessment.

All candidates must complete a 15 minute tutorial before the assessment begins and will have the opportunity to familiarise themselves with the calculator and practice using it.

Candidates may practise using the calculator by downloading and installing the practice exam at http://www.vue.com/athena/ . The calculator can be accessed from the fourth sample question (of 12).

Please note that the practice exam and tutorial provided by Pearson VUE at http://www.vue.com/athena/ is not specific to CIMA and includes the full range of question types the Pearson VUE software supports, some of which CIMA does not currently use.

F FUNDAMENTALS OF FINANCIAL ACCOUNTING AND COMPUTER-BASED ASSESSMENT

The assessment for Fundamentals of Financial Accounting is a 120 minute computer-based assessment comprising 50 compulsory questions. CIMA is continuously developing the question styles within the CBA system and you are advised to try the online website demo at www.cimaglobal.com, to both gain familiarity with assessment software and examine the latest style of questions being used.

G SYLLABUS OUTLINE

Syllabus overview

The main objective of this paper is the preparation of financial statements for single entities. These statements are constructed within a conceptual and regulatory framework requiring an understanding of the various valuation alternatives, the role of legislation and of accounting standards. Being able to apply accounting techniques and systems enables the preparation of accounts for different types of operations and for specific transactions. There is an introduction to measuring financial performance with the calculation of basic ratios. The need to understand and apply necessary controls for accounting systems, looking at internal control and the nature of errors and fraud, is also covered.

Note: students are required to be aware of the format and content of published accounts but are not required to prepare them. No knowledge of any specific accounting treatment contained in the International Financial Reporting Standards (IFRSs) – including the International Accounting Standards (IASs), – is necessary, except in terms of how they influence the presentation of financial statements. IAS 1 and IAS 7 formats will form the basis of those statements. The terminology used for all entities will be that seen in the International Financial Reporting Standards. This will enable students to use a consistent set of accounting terms throughout their studies.

Also note that IAS1 allows the presentation of income in the form of a single statement of comprehensive income or as two separate statements, an income statement and a statement of comprehensive income. Because of the nature of the material dealt with at this level, the majority of questions on this topic will ask for income statement format. However students must be aware of the layout of the single statement of comprehensive income and be able to use it if required.

Syllabus structure

The syllabus comprises the following topics and study weightings:

A	Conceptual and regulatory framework	20%
B	Accounting systems	20%
C	Preparation of accounts for single entities	45%
D	Control of accounting systems	15%

Assessment strategy

There will be a two hour computer based assessment, comprising 50 compulsory questions, each with one or more parts.

A variety of objective test question styles and types will be used within the assessment.

C02 – A. CONCEPTUAL AND REGULATORY FRAMEWORK (20%)

Learning outcomes
On completion of their studies students should be able to:

Lead	Component	Level	Indicative syllabus content
1. explain the concepts of financial accounting.	(a) explain the need for accounting records; [1] (b) identify user groups and the characteristics of financial statements; [1] (c) distinguish between financial and management accounts; [1] (d) identify the underlying assumptions, policies and changes in accounting estimates; [10] (e) explain capital and revenue, cash and profit, income and expenditure, assets and liabilities; [2] (f) distinguish between tangible and intangible assets; [6] (g) explain the historical cost convention; [10] (h) identify alternative methods of valuing assets, and their impact on profit measures and statement of financial position values. [6], [10]	2 2 2 2 2 2 2 2	• Accounting records. [1] • Users of accounts and the objectives and the qualitative characteristics of financial statements. [1] • Functions of financial and management accounts; purpose of accounting statements; stewardship; the accounting equation. [1], [2] • Underlying assumptions, policies, changes in accounting estimates; capital and revenue; cash and profit; income, expenditure, assets and liabilities. [10] • Tangible and intangible assets. [6] • Historical cost convention. [10] • Asset valuation including current cost, fair value and value in use bases and their implications for profit measurement and the statement of financial position. [6], [10]
2. explain the regulatory and legal framework for financial accounting.	(a) explain the influence of legislation on published accounting information for organisations; [10] (b) explain the role of accounting standards in preparing financial statements; [10] (c) explain approaches to creating accounting standards. [10]	2 2 2	• Regulatory influence of company law (e.g. Companies Acts, EC directives); items in formats for published accounts. [10] • Role of accounting standards in financial statements. [10] • Principles and rules based approaches to creating accounting standards. [10]

C02 – B. ACCOUNTING SYSTEMS (20%)

Learning outcomes
On completion of their studies students should be able to:

Lead	Component	Level	Indicative syllabus content
1. prepare ledger accounts and supporting documents.	(a) explain the principles of double-entry bookkeeping; [3]	2	• Ledger accounts; double-entry bookkeeping. [3]
	(b) prepare cash and bank accounts, and bank reconciliation statements; [3], [9]	3	• Accounts for cash and bank, bank reconciliations, imprest system for petty cash. [3]
	(c) prepare petty cash statements under an imprest system; [8]	3	• Accounts for sales and purchases, including personal accounts and control accounts. [3], [8], [9]
	(d) prepare accounts for sales and purchases, including personal accounts and control accounts; [3], [8], [9]	3	• Nominal ledger accounts and journal entries. [3], [8]
	(e) prepare nominal ledger accounts, journal entries and a trial balance; [3], [4], [8]	3	• Trial balance. [4]
	(f) prepare accounts for indirect taxes; [5]	3	• Accounts for indirect taxes e.g. value added tax, sales tax. [5]
	(g) prepare accounts for payroll; [5]	3	• Accounts for payroll. [5]
	(h) prepare a non-current asset register. [6]	3	• Non-current asset register. [6]
2. explain the use of codes in accounting systems.	(a) explain the need for accounting codes; [9]	2	• Accounting codes and their uses. [9]
	(b) illustrate the use of simple coding systems. [9]	2	

C02 – C. PREPARATION OF ACCOUNTS FOR SINGLE ENTITIES (45%)

Learning outcomes
On completion of their studies students should be able to:

Lead	Component	Level	Indicative syllabus content
1. prepare accounts for transactions.	(a) prepare accounts using accruals and prepayments; [5]	3	• Adjustments to the trial balance; accruals and prepayments. [5]
	(b) prepare accounts for bad debts and allowances for receivables; [5]	3	• Bad debts and allowances for receivables. [5]
	(c) prepare accounts using different methods of calculating depreciation and for impairment values; [6]	3	• Accounting treatment for depreciation (straight line, reducing balance and revaluation methods) and impairment. [6]
	(d) prepare accounts for inventories; [8]	3	• Accounts for inventories (excluding construction contracts); methods of inventory measurement (FIFO, LIFO and average cost). [8]
	(e) prepare manufacturing accounts; [12]	3	• Manufacturing accounts. [12]
	(f) prepare income and expenditure accounts; [11]	3	• Income and expenditure accounts. [11]
	(g) prepare accounts from incomplete records; [11]	3	• Accounting statements from incomplete data. [11]
	(h) prepare accounts for the issue and redemption of shares and debentures. [13]	3	• Accounts for the Issue and redemption of shares and debentures. [13]

Learning outcomes
On completion of their studies students should be able to:

Lead	Component	Level	Indicative syllabus content
2. prepare financial statements for a single entity.	(a) prepare financial statements from trial balance; [7], [13] (b) prepare a statement of cash flows. [13]	3 3	• Income statement, statement of comprehensive income and statement of financial position; statement of changes in equity. [13] • Statement of cash flows. [13]
3. demonstrate the use of basic ratios in financial performance.	(a) calculate basic ratios. [14]	3	• Ratios: return on capital employed; gross and net profit margins; asset turnover; trade receivables collection period and trade payables payment period; current and quick ratios; inventory turnover; gearing. [14]

C02 – D. CONTROL OF ACCOUNTING SYSTEMS (15%)

Learning outcomes
On completion of their studies students should be able to:

Lead	Component	Level	Indicative syllabus content
1. explain the need for external controls on a business.	(a) identify the requirements for external audit and the basic processes undertaken; [10] (b) explain the meaning of fair presentation; [10] (c) distinguish between external and internal audit. [10]	2 2 2	• External audit. [10] • Fair presentation. [10] • Distinction between external and internal audit. [10]
2. explain internal control techniques.	(a) explain the purpose and basic procedures of internal audit; [10] (b) explain the need for financial controls; [10] (c) explain the purpose of audit checks and audit trails; [10]	2 2 2	• Internal audit. [10] • Financial controls, audit checks and audit trails. [10]
3. demonstrate how accounting errors are corrected.	(a) explain the nature of accounting errors; [4] (b) prepare accounting entries for the correction of errors; [9]	2 3	• Errors including those of principle, omission, and commission. [4] • Journal entries and suspense accounts [9]
4. explain the nature of fraud.	(a) explain the nature of fraud; [10] (b) explain the basic methods of fraud prevention and detection. [10]	2 2	• Types of fraud. [10] • Methods for prevention of fraud including levels of authorisation, documentation and staff organisation. [10] • Methods of detection of fraud including spot checks, comparison with external evidence, reconciliations and control accounts. [10]

EXAMINATION TECHNIQUES

COMPUTER-BASED ASSESSMENT

TEN GOLDEN RULES

1   Make sure you are familiar with the software before you start exam. You cannot speak to the invigilator once you have started.

2   These exam practice kits give you plenty of exam style questions to practise.

3   Attempt all questions, there is no negative marking.

4   Double check your answer before you put in the final answer.

5   On multiple choice questions (MCQs), there is only one correct answer.

6   Not all questions will be MCQs – you may have to fill in missing words or figures.

7   Identify the easy questions first and get some points on the board to build up your confidence.

8   Try and allow 15 minutes at the end to check your answers and make any corrections.

9   If you don't know the answer, try a process of elimination.

10   Work out your answer on paper first if it is easier for you. Scrap paper will be provided for you. You are allowed to take pens, pencils and rulers with you to the examination, but you are not allowed pencil cases, phones, paper or notes, or a calculator.

Section 1

PRACTICE QUESTIONS

THE ACCOUNTING SCENE

SYNOPSIS

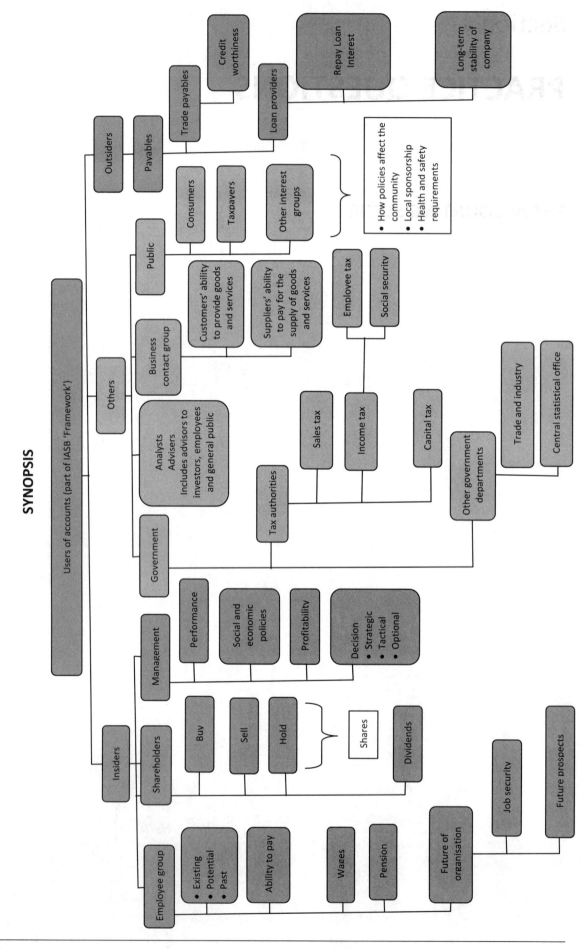

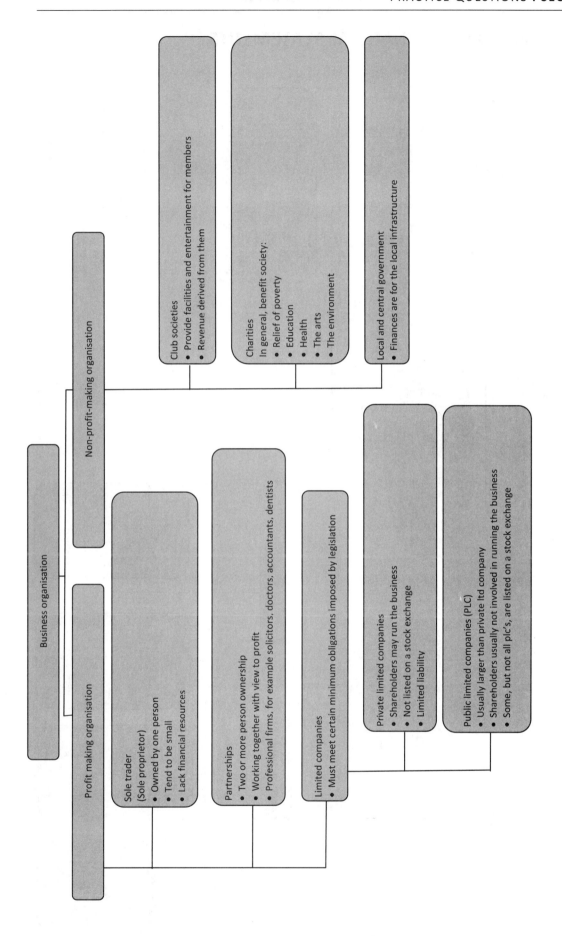

Business organisation

Profit making organisation

Sole trader
(Sole proprietor)
- Owned by one person
- Tend to be small
- Lack financial resources

Partnerships
- Two or more person ownership
- Working together with view to profit
- Professional firms, for example solicitors, doctors, accountants, dentists

Limited companies
- Must meet certain minimum obligations imposed by legislation

Private limited companies
- Shareholders may run the business
- Not listed on a stock exchange
- Limited liability

Public limited companies (PLC)
- Usually larger than private ltd company
- Shareholders usually not involved in running the business
- Some, but not all plc's, are listed on a stock exchange

Non-profit-making organisation

Club societies
- Provide facilities and entertainment for members
- Revenue derived from them

Charities
In general, benefit society:
- Relief of poverty
- Education
- Health
- The arts
- The environment

Local and central government
- Finances are for the local infrastructure

THE FRAMEWORK OF FINANCIAL STATEMENTS

SYNOPSIS

The accounting equation

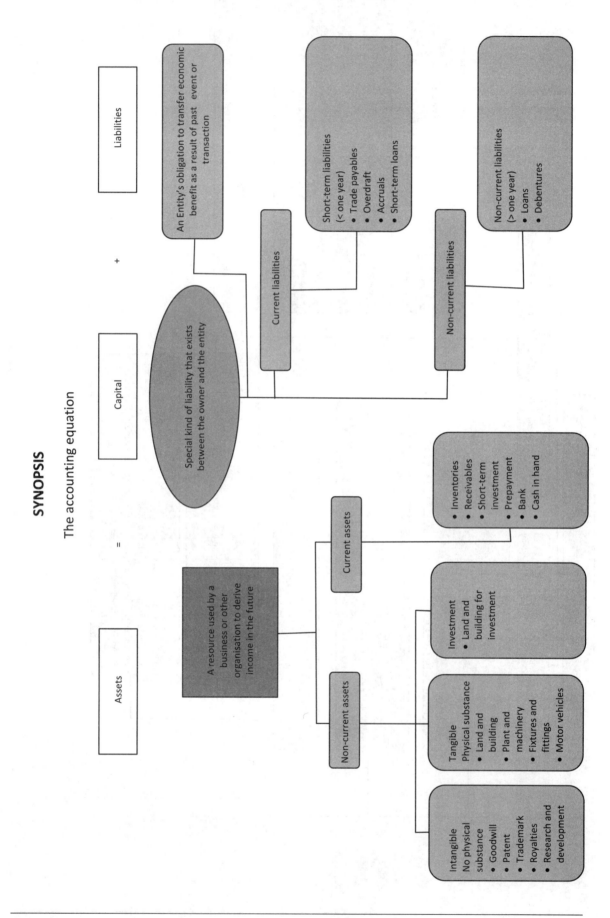

The statement of financial position is presented as the accounting equation, but in a vertical format. Thus:

Assets	X
	——
Capital	X
Liabilities	X
	——
	X
	——

The income statement

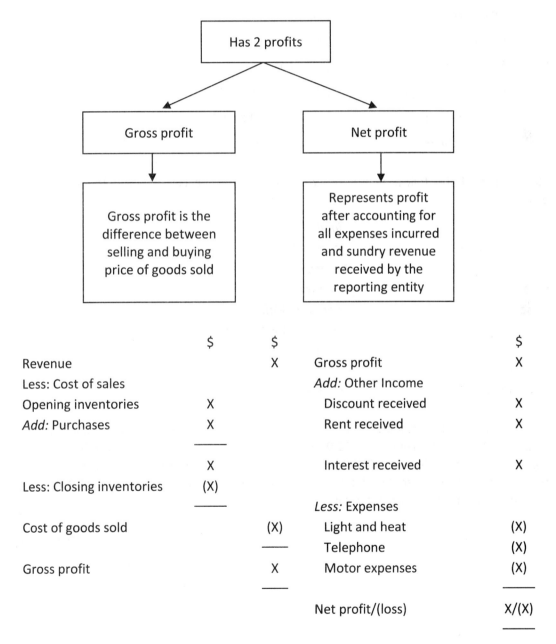

	$	$		$
Revenue		X	Gross profit	X
Less: Cost of sales			*Add:* Other Income	
Opening inventories	X		Discount received	X
Add: Purchases	X		Rent received	X
	——			
	X		Interest received	X
Less: Closing inventories	(X)			
	——		*Less:* Expenses	
Cost of goods sold		(X)	Light and heat	(X)
		——	Telephone	(X)
Gross profit		X	Motor expenses	(X)
		——		——
			Net profit/(loss)	X/(X)
				——

1

	Assets	Liabilities	Capital
	$	$	$
(i)	50,000	7,200	?
(ii)	112,000	19,600	?
(iii)	67,200	?	50,000
(iv)	96,400	?	65,800
(v)	?	25,200	76,800
(vi)	?	50,600	159,000

Fill in the blanks (?) in the table above.

2   Classify the following into Assets and Liabilities.

(i)	Bank balance	(vii)	Premises
(ii)	We owe for goods	(viii)	Trade payable
(iii)	Motor vehicle	(ix)	Loan from D Randle
(iv)	Fixture and fittings	(x)	Cash in hand
(v)	Loan from Pringle	(xi)	Owing to bank
(vi)	Office machinery	(xii)	Receivables

3   State which of the following are shown under the wrong classification for Kapil Dev's business.

Assets	Liabilities
Loan from A Lamb	Receivables
Motor vehicles	Money owing to bank
Premises	Inventories
Goodwill	Loan from Riffle
Machinery	Money owing to A Little
Cash in hand	Fixtures
Capital	Payables
Cash at bank	Buildings

4   Mark Waugh starts in business. Before any sales, he has purchased fixtures $12,000, motor vehicle $30,000 and inventories $21,000. Although he has paid in full for the fixtures and motor vehicle, he still owes $8,400 for some of the inventory. His brother Steve has lent him $18,000. Mark, after the above, has $16,800 in the business bank account and $600 cash in hand. Calculate Mark's capital?

THE ACCOUNTING SYSTEM IN ACTION

SYNOPSIS

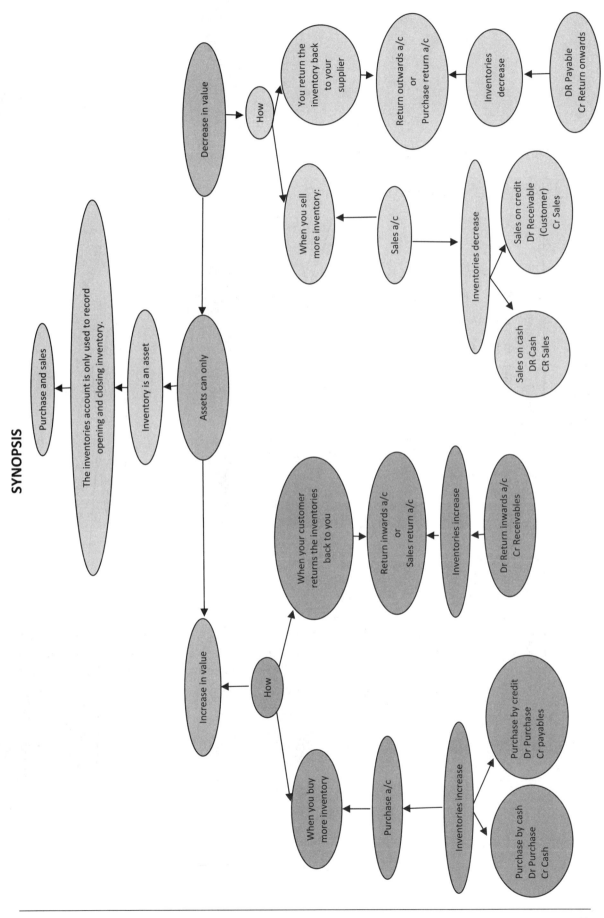

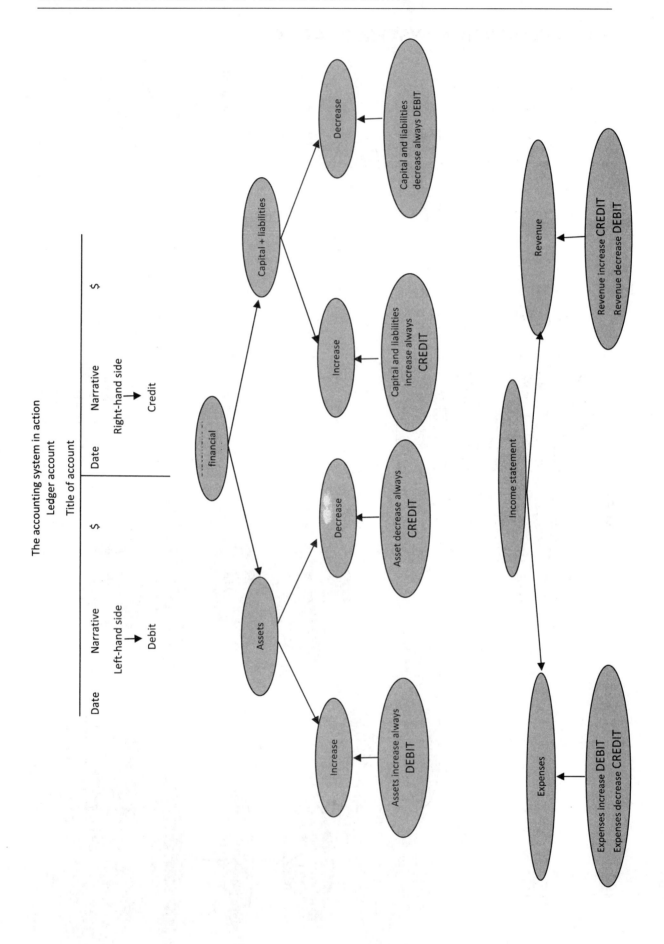

5   Tick the correct boxes for the following:

		Debit	Credit
(i)	Increase in assets		
(ii)	Increase in capital		
(iii)	Decrease in capital		
(iv)	Increase in liabilities		
(v)	Decrease in assets		
(vi)	Decrease in liabilities		
(vii)	Increase in expenses		
(viii)	Decrease in revenue		
(ix)	Decrease in expenses		
(x)	Increase in revenue		

6   Complete the table showing which accounts are to be credited and which are to be debited. Consider all items below as INVENTORIES.

		Account to be debited	Account to be credited
(i)	Goods bought on credit from S Davis		
(ii)	Goods returned to us by H Higgins		
(iii)	Machinery returned to A Snooker Ltd		
(iv)	Goods bought for cash		
(v)	Motor van bought on credit from I Landle		
(vi)	Goods returned by us to B Boro		
(vii)	J McEnroe paid up his account by cheque		
(viii)	Goods bought by cheque		
(ix)	We paid payable, S Graf, by cheque		
(x)	Goods sold on credit to J Muller		

7   SPORT STARS

Please prepare T accounts for the transactions below.

Comprehensive example (Sport stars)

20X4

September 1	Bought goods on credit $68 from D Underwood
September 2	Bought goods on credit $154 from M Hughes
September 5	Sold goods on credit to A Border for $60
September 6	Sold goods on credit to A Steward for $50
September 10	Returned goods $14 to D Underwood
September 12	Goods bought for cash $100
September 19	A Steward returned goods $16 to us
September 21	Goods sold for cash $150
September 22	Paid cash to D Underwood $54
September 30	A Border paid the amount owing by him $60 in cash
September 30	Bought goods on credit $128 from M Hughes

SUMMARISING THE LEDGER ACCOUNTS

SYNOPSIS

The following errors do not prevent the trial balance from agreeing

Error of omission

Where the transaction has been completely omitted from the ledger accounts

Error of commission

Where one side of the transaction has been entered in the wrong account, but of the correct type, e.g. expense, revenue, asset, liability, capital (will not affect profit or statement of financial position)

Error of principle

As for errors of commission, but the correct and incorrect accounts are of different types, e.g. entered in purchase account instead of non-current asset account (will affect profit and statement of financial position)

Error of original entry

Where the wrong amount has been used for both debit and credit side

Reversal of entry

Where the debit has been made to the account that should have been credited and vice versa

Duplication of entries

Where the transaction has been posted twice

Compensation errors

Where two or more transactions have been entered incorrectly, but cancelling each other out, e.g. wages debited with $200 in excess and sale credited with $200 in excess

From ledger accounts to financial statements

Bank A/C

18 Dec 2001 SP A/C	30	16 Dec 2001 Rent	40
31 Dec 2001 Bal c/d	80	18 Dec 2001 Furniture	70
	110		110
		1 Jan 2002 Bal b/d	80

Furniture

18 Dec 2001 Bank	70	31 Dec Bal c/d	70
	70		70
1 Jan 2002 Bal b/d	70		

SP A/C

31 Dec 2001 Bal c/d	30	18 Dec 2001 Bank	30
	30		30
		1 Jan 2002 Bal b/d	30

Rent A/C

16 Dec 2001 Bank	40	31 Dec 2001 Bal c/d	40
	40		40
1 Jan 2002 Bal b/d	40		

Prepare trial balance

Trial balance as at 31 December 2001

	DR $	CR $
Bank A/C		80
Furniture A/C	70	
SP A/C		30
Rent A/C	40	
	110	110

Income statement

Statement of financial position

The trial balance

It is a list of balances in a double entry bookkeeping system. If the records have been correctly maintained, the sum of the debit balances will equal the sum of the credit balances although certain errors, such as errors of omission of transaction or erroneous entries, will not be disclosed by the trial balance.

Trial balance is thus a list of balances on the ledger accounts. If the totals of the debit and credit balances on the trial balance are not equal, then an error or errors have been made either

(a)   in the posting of the transactions to the ledger accounts or

(b)   in the balancing of the accounts or

(c)   in the transferring of the balances from the ledger account to the trial balance.

8   What is the definition of a trial balance?

9   State THREE reasons why a trial balance may not balance?

10   Give four examples of errors that do not affect the trial balance from agreeing and explain what each one means.

FURTHER ASPECTS OF LEDGER ACCOUNTS

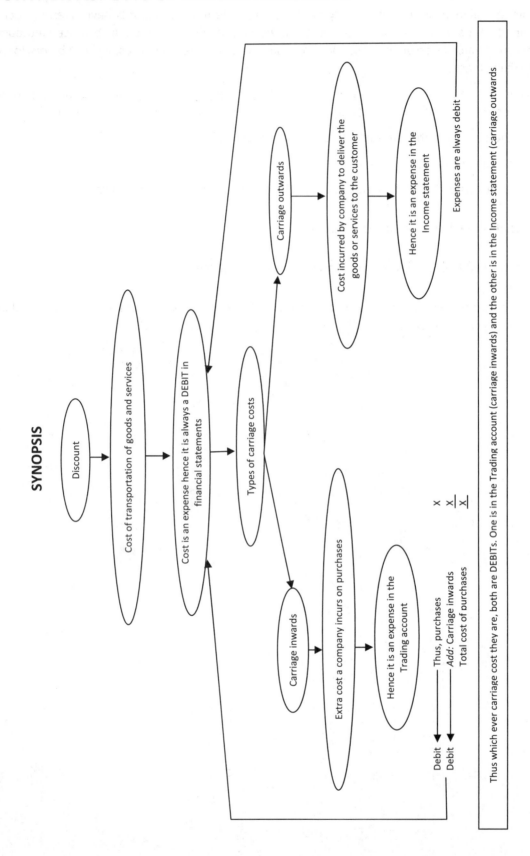

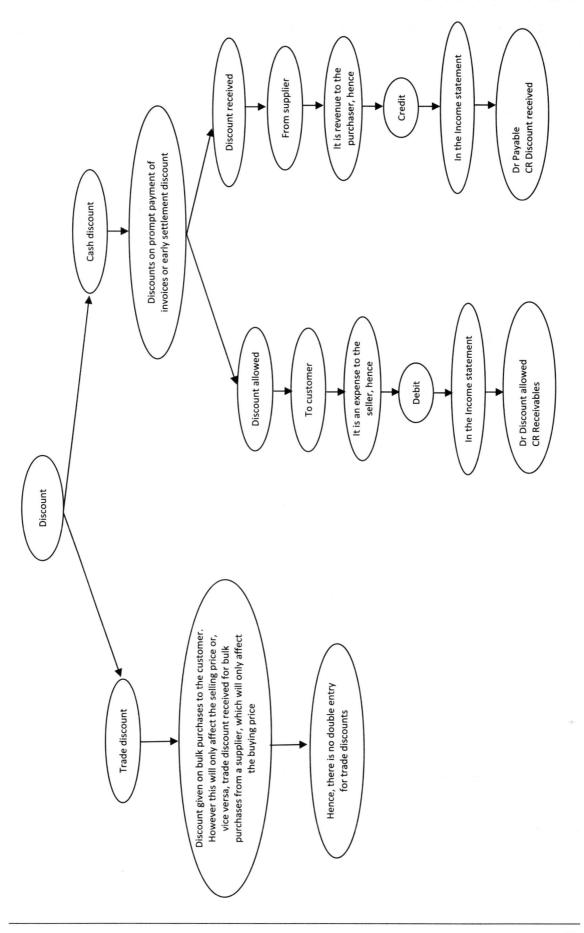

ACCOUNTING FOR SALES TAX

When an organisation reaches a certain level of revenue then they are obliged to register with the tax authorities. There are normally two rates of sales tax and exemption:

- Standard rate
- Zero rate
- Exempt

Sales tax on sales is classified as output tax.

Sales tax on purchases is classified as input tax.

Examples

1   Purchase goods costing $360 subject to 20% trade discount:

	$
List price	360.00
Less: Trade discount 20%	72.00
Net goods value	288.00
Sales tax @ 17½%	50.40
	338.40

Entries:

		$	$
Dr	Purchases	288.00	
Dr	Sales tax	50.40	
Cr	Supplier		338.40

2   Sold goods costing $80:

	$
Sales	80.00
Sales tax 17½%	14.00
Total Sales	94.00

		$	$
Dr	Receivables	94.00	
Cr	Sales		80.00
Cr	Sales tax		14.00

3   Gross amount of $500, calculate sales tax on this figure if the rate of sales tax is 17½%:

$500 × 17.5/(100 + 17.5) = $74.47

Hence sales are $500 − $74.47 = $425.53

ACCRUALS AND PREPAYMENTS

With any expense account, always ask the following questions to determine an accrual or a prepayment.

(a)   How much am I suppose to pay? and

(b)   How much have I paid?

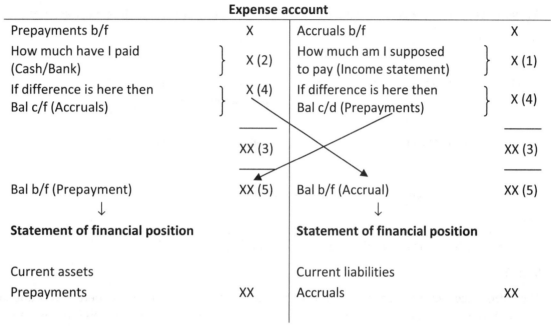

Expense account

Prepayments b/f	X	Accruals b/f	X
How much have I paid (Cash/Bank)	X (2)	How much am I supposed to pay (Income statement)	X (1)
If difference is here then Bal c/f (Accruals)	X (4)	If difference is here then Bal c/d (Prepayments)	X (4)
	XX (3)		XX (3)
Bal b/f (Prepayment)	XX (5)	Bal b/f (Accrual)	XX (5)

Statement of financial position ↓   Statement of financial position ↓

Current assets		Current liabilities	
Prepayments	XX	Accruals	XX

(1)–(5) represents orders of transaction.

With any Revenue account, always ask the following questions?

(a)   How much am I suppose to receive? and

(b)   How much have I received?

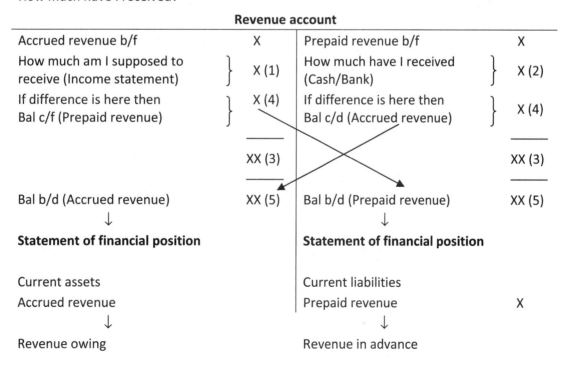

Revenue account

Accrued revenue b/f	X	Prepaid revenue b/f	X
How much am I supposed to receive (Income statement)	X (1)	How much have I received (Cash/Bank)	X (2)
If difference is here then Bal c/f (Prepaid revenue)	X (4)	If difference is here then Bal c/d (Accrued revenue)	X (4)
	XX (3)		XX (3)
Bal b/d (Accrued revenue)	XX (5)	Bal b/d (Prepaid revenue)	XX (5)

Statement of financial position ↓   Statement of financial position ↓

Current assets		Current liabilities	
Accrued revenue		Prepaid revenue	X
↓		↓	
Revenue owing		Revenue in advance	

STEP BY STEP GUIDE ON HOW TO DEAL WITH ACCRUALS AND PREPAYMENTS.

Step1

Ask yourself, is there any expense or revenue balances brought forward from previous years – hence always check the DATES carefully to determine this.

Step 2

Ask yourself, is there any amounts that I am suppose to pay or receive (Income statement entry).

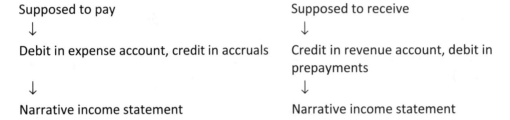

Supposed to pay	Supposed to receive
↓	↓
Debit in expense account, credit in accruals	Credit in revenue account, debit in prepayments
↓	↓
Narrative income statement	Narrative income statement

Step 3

Ask yourself how much has been paid or received.

Step 4

Calculate the totals on either the expense or revenue account.

Step 5

The difference will represent the accrual/prepayment expense in the expense account or the accrued revenue/prepaid revenue in the revenue account. The accruals/prepayments and accrued revenue/prepaid revenue will be the closing balances for the year.

Expense account		Revenue account	
Accruals	Prepayments	Accrued revenue	Prepaid revenue
↓	↓	↓	↓
Debit c/d	Credit c/d	Credit c/d	Debit c/d
↓	↓	↓	↓
Credit b/d	Debit b/d	Debit b/d	Credit b/d

BAD DEBTS AND ALLOWANCES FOR RECEIVABLES

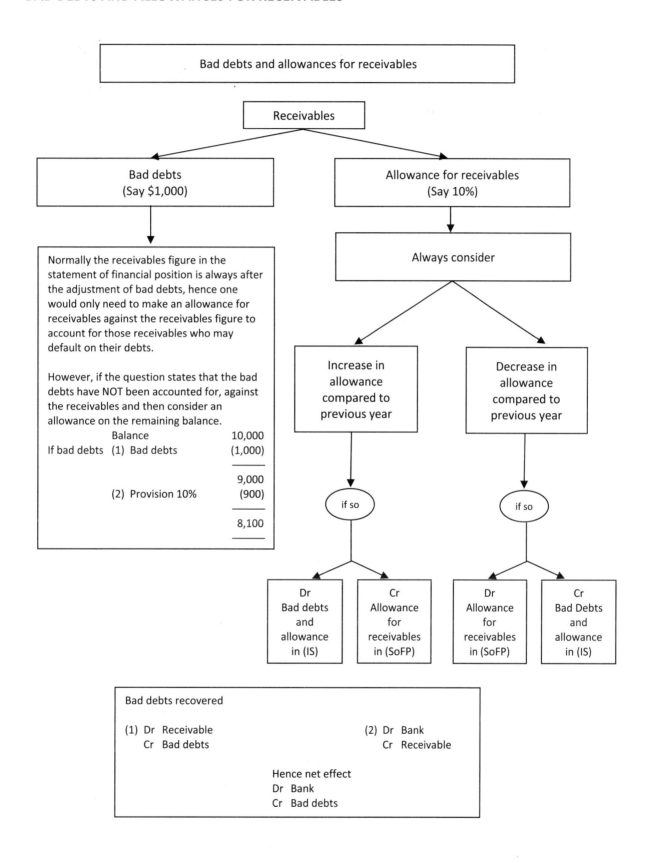

WAGES AND SALARIES

Gross Pay is the amount due to an employee before deductions. Deductions may be compulsory, e.g. tax and social security, and optional, e.g. pension contributions.

The amount paid to an employee after deductions is the Net Pay.

The cost to an employer of salaries is the Gross Pay, PLUS any amounts in addition which the employer has to pay, or chooses to pay. For example, an employer may have to pay employer's social security, and may choose to make a voluntary contribution to an employee's pension scheme.

The charge to the income statement is thus Gross Pay, PLUS employer's social security, PLUS employer's pension contribution, where applicable.

The amounts deducted from an employee's gross pay, e.g. tax and employee's social security, and the employer's 'add-ons', e.g. employers social security, may not be paid over to the relevant authority immediately. Where this is the case, these amounts will be credited to a Wages and Control account and debited to that account when paid, just like any other liability.

ACCOUNTING FOR NON-CURRENT ASSETS

SYNOPSIS

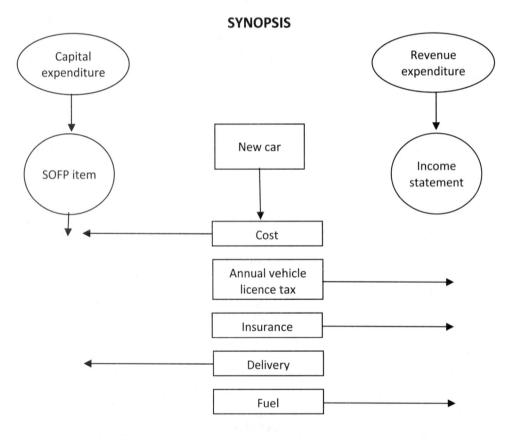

Why statement of financial position?
Material amount in ($) (cost of car)

Lasts long-term (> 1 year)
Delivery cost is part of the cost of the car

Why income statement?
Annual expense necessary to use the asset (e.g. annual vehicle licence tax, insurance)

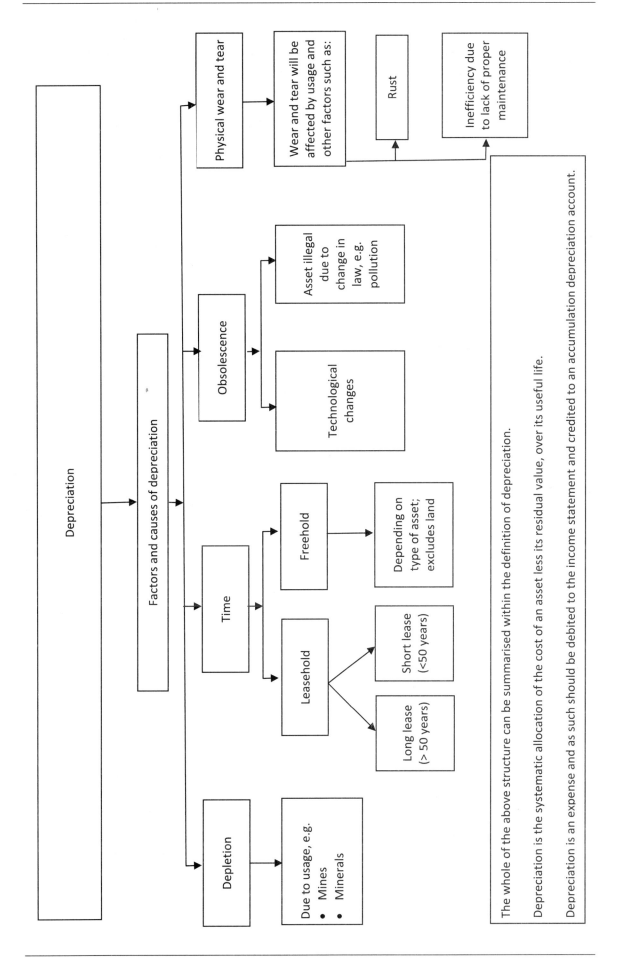

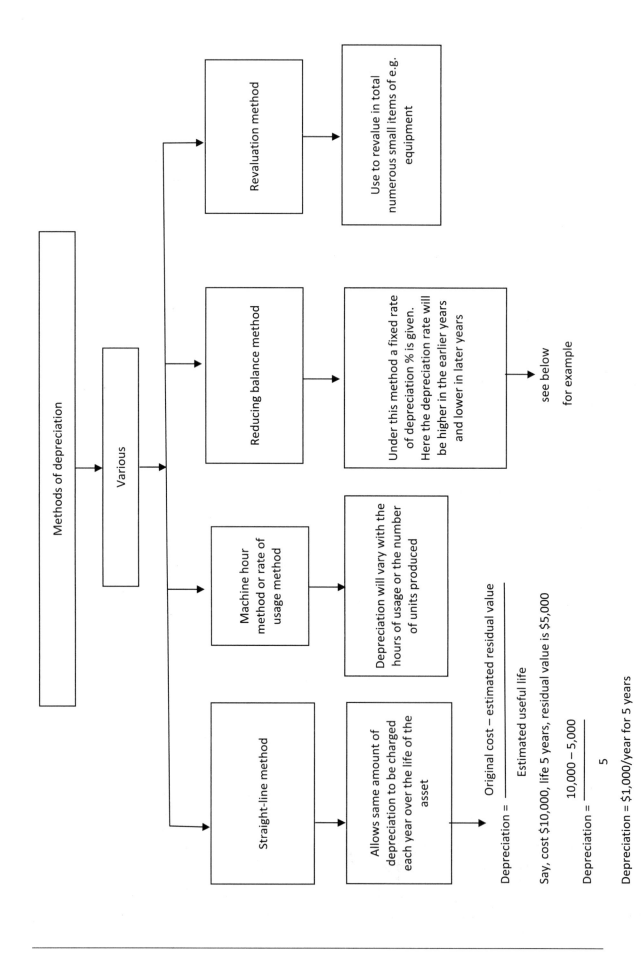

Purchase and sale of non-current assets; Accounting treatment

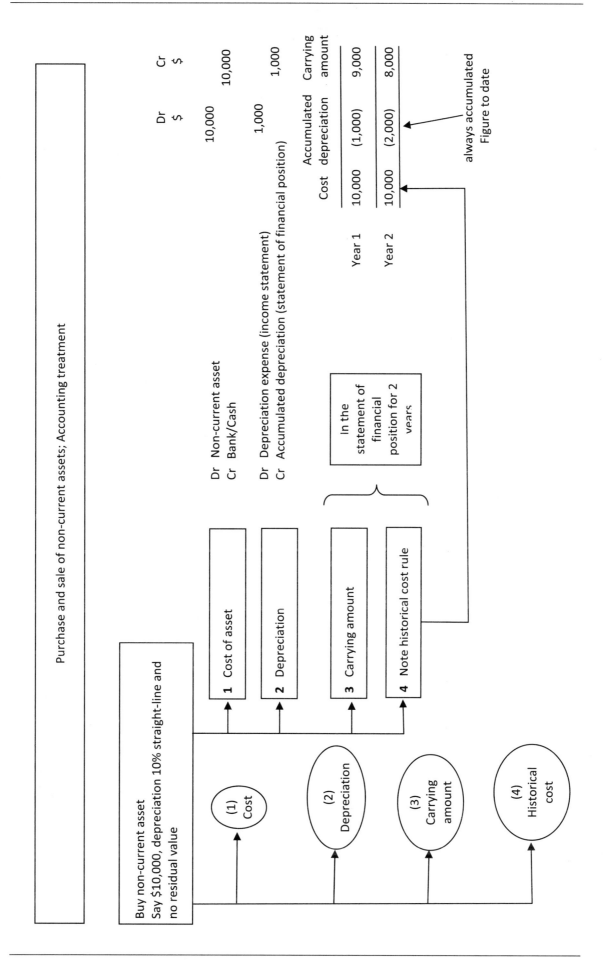

Buy non-current asset
Say $10,000, depreciation 10% straight-line and
no residual value

		Dr $	Cr $
Dr	Non-current asset	10,000	
Cr	Bank/Cash		10,000
Dr	Depreciation expense (income statement)	1,000	
Cr	Accumulated depreciation (statement of financial position)		1,000

	Cost	Accumulated depreciation	Carrying amount
Year 1	10,000	(1,000)	9,000
Year 2	10,000	(2,000)	8,000

always accumulated
Figure to date

(1) Cost — **1** Cost of asset

(2) Depreciation — **2** Depreciation

(3) Carrying amount — **3** Carrying amount

In the statement of financial position for 2 years

(4) Historical cost — **4** Note historical cost rule

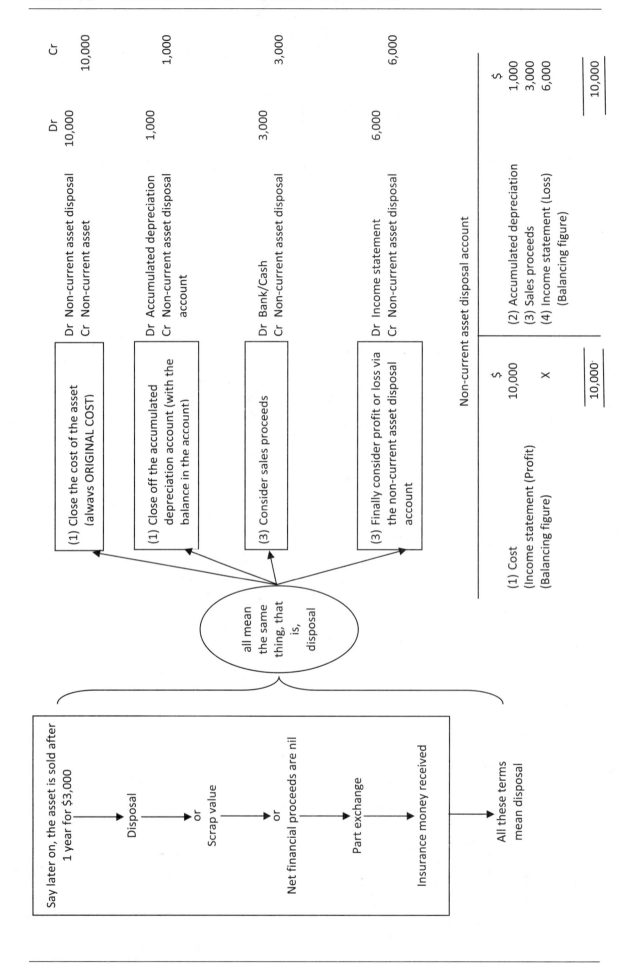

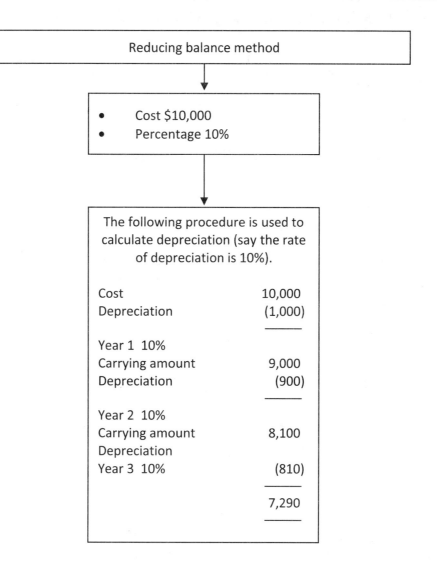

Reducing balance method

- Cost $10,000
- Percentage 10%

The following procedure is used to calculate depreciation (say the rate of depreciation is 10%).

Cost	10,000
Depreciation	(1,000)
	_____
Year 1 10%	
Carrying amount	9,000
Depreciation	(900)
	_____
Year 2 10%	
Carrying amount	8,100
Depreciation	
Year 3 10%	(810)
	_____
	7,290
	_____

When dealing with non-current assets and the calculation of depreciation you must always carry out the calculations in a methodical manner.
Hence,

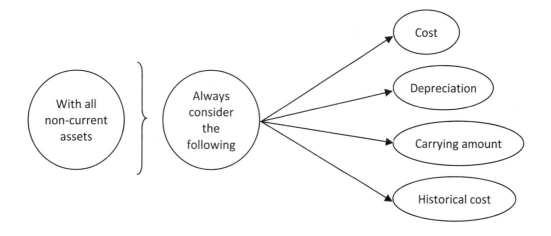

In the statement of financial position, depreciation is shown as follows:

	Cost $	Accumulated depreciation $	Carrying amount $
Say, depreciation is at 10% straight line			
Year 1	10,000	(1,000)	9,000
Year 2	9,000	(1,000)	8,000

This is INCORRECT. Why?

	Cost	Accumulated depreciation	Carrying amount
Thus			
Year 2	10,000	(2,000)	8,000

Correct method

1,000 last year

1,000 current year

11 State FOUR methods for calculating depreciation.

12 When a non-current is purchased for cash what is the journal entry?

A	Dr	Asset	Cr	Bank
B	Dr	Bank	Cr	Asset
C	Dr	Purchase	Cr	Bank
D	Dr	Bank	Cr	Purchase

13 What is the double entry for disposal of a non-current asset, where the NCA is sold for a profit?

	Dr $	Cr $
Cost of NCA		
Cum Depn NCA		
Bank		
Disposal account		

PREPARATION OF FINANCIAL STATEMENTS WITH ADJUSTMENTS

SYNOPSIS

In previous chapters, you have learnt about the:

- Trial balance
- Adjustments to the trial balance for:
  - Inventories
  - Accruals
  - Prepayments
  - Depreciation
  - Allowance for receivables
- The preparation of:
  - Income statement
  - Statement of financial position

This chapter is your chance to 'put it all together' and to produce financial statements from a trial balance with adjustments.

This chapter has only two large questions. Whilst you will not see a question like this in the computer-based assessment (CBA), this question will help you see how everything fits into place. CBA questions only focus on one small part of a large question like this, but seeing the 'big picture' should help you answer small detailed questions.

14 The trial balance of NICO, a sole proprietor, for the year ended 31 July 20X9 was as follows:

	$	$
Capital		100,000
Plant and machinery:		
Cost	155,000	
Accumulated depreciation to 1 August 20X8		50,000
Trade receivables	15,000	
Trade payables		3,000
Inventories at 1 August 20X8	10,000	
Cash at bank	3,400	
Sales		150,000
Drawings	35,000	
Allowance for receivables at 1 August 20X8		2,000
Bank loan – repayable 2015		20,000
Purchases	40,000	
Selling and distribution expenses	50,000	
Administration expenses	15,000	
Interest	1,600	
	_____	_____
	325,000	325,000
	_____	_____

The following final adjustments are required:

(i)   inventories at 31 July 20X9 were valued at $12,000

(ii)   selling and distribution expenses of $4,000 are to be accrued

(iii)   administration expenses of $6,000 were prepaid.

(iv)   the allowance for receivables is to be adjusted to 5% of receivables.

(v)   depreciation on the plant and machinery is $15,000 for the year to 31 July 20X9.

Requirements:

Prepare an income statement for the year ended 31 July 20X9 and a statement of financial position at that date.

15   Fletcher is a sole proprietor trading as A1 Alarms. The trial balance of A1 Alarms at 31 August 20X3 is set out below.

	Dr	Cr
	$	$
Advertising	8,000	
Bank	2,000	
Bank loan		20,000
Bank interest	2,000	
Capital		20,000
Capital introduced		5,000
Carriage outwards	12,000	
Computing expenses	10,000	
Payables		20,000
Receivables	30,000	
Discount received		3,000
Drawings	33,000	
Fixtures at cost	60,000	
Power	4,000	
Accumulated depreciation on fixtures at 1 September 20X2		15,000
Allowance for receivables at 1 September 20X2		2,000
Purchases	240,000	
Rent	6,000	
Salaries	36,000	
Sales		382,000
Inventories at 1 September 20X2	24,000	
	467,000	467,000

The following additional information was provided.

(i)   The inventories at 31 August 20X3 were valued at $20,000

(ii)   The prepayment for rent at 31 August 20X3 was $2,000

(iii)   The accrual for power was $1,000

(iv)   The computer crashed in August 20X3. An engineer gave an estimate of $500 to repair the computer, which Fletcher accepted. The engineer repaired the computer in August 20X3 but has not yet submitted his invoice.

(v)   Deprecation is to be provided for the year ended 31 August 20X3 on the fixtures on the reducing balance basis at 33% per annum.

(vi)   The allowance for receivables is to be 5% of the receivables.

Required:

Prepare the financial statements for A1 Alarms for the year ended 31 August 20X3.

ORGANISING THE BOOKKEEPING SYSTEM

SYNOPSIS

Books of prime entry include the following:

(i)   Sales day book or Sales journal or Sales book

(ii)   Purchases day book or Purchase journal or Purchase book

(iii)   Journals

(iv)   Cash book

(v)   Petty cash book

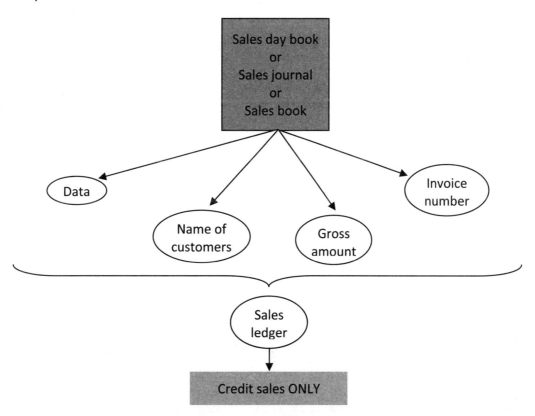

Cash book and Petty cash book are books of prime entry and are also part of the double entry system

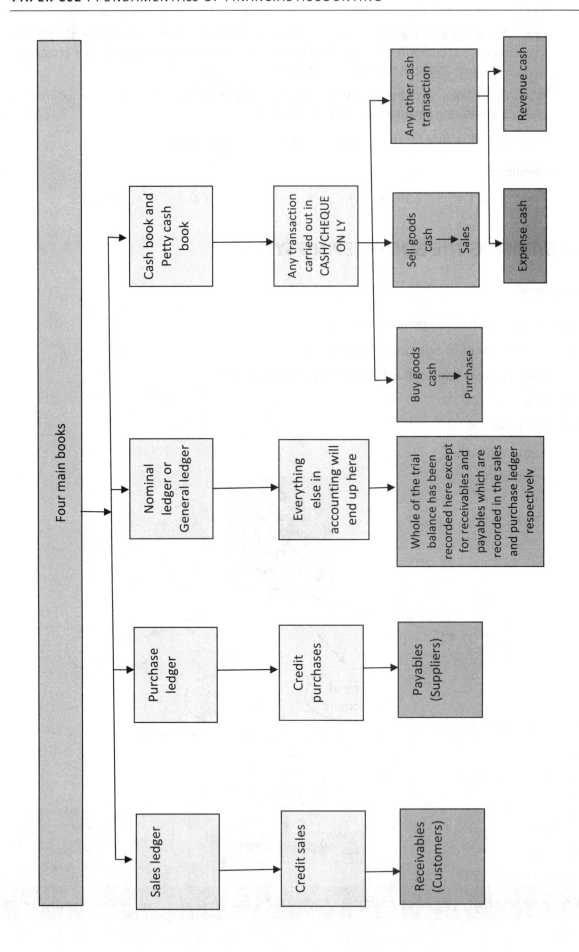

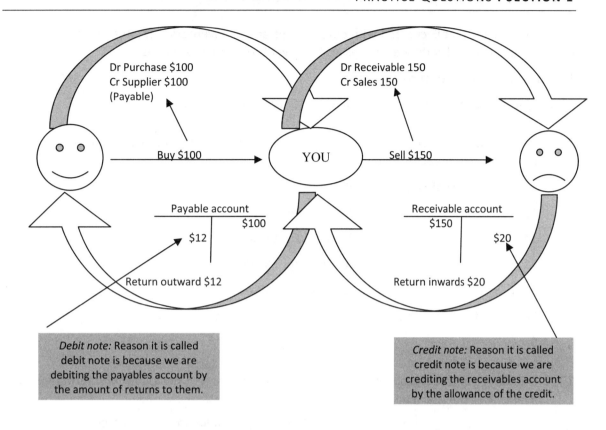

Jeremy goes to Esso petrol station and spends $100 using his American Express. American Express charge 10% commission on all such transactions. Show the entries from the initial sale to final receipt of cash from Esso's point of view.

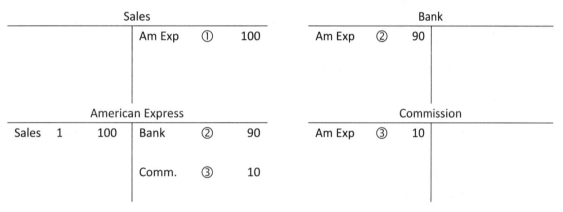

Inventory measurement

Inventories valued at the lower of cost and net realisable value

Cost = cost of goods + carriage inwards, or manufactured cost

NRV = selling price less any disposal costs

Methods of inventory measurement

First In, First Out   FIFO

Last In, First Out   LIFO

Average Cost   AVCO

FIFO – this means that IS charged with oldest prices and BS inventories at latest prices LIFO – this means that IS charged with latest prices and BS inventories at oldest prices

This means that in times of rising prices:

FIFO – gives a higher profit and higher inventories valuation than LIFO

16 A firm uses the LIFO cost formula. Information regarding inventories movements during a particular month are as follows:

1	Opening balance	300 units valued at $3,000
10	Purchases	700 units for $8,400
14	Sales	400 units for $8,000
21	Purchases	600 units for $9,000
23	Sales	800 units for $17,600

The cost of inventories at the end of the month would be:

$ _____

17 S & Co. sells three products – Small, Medium and Large. The following information was available at the year-end:

	Small	Medium	Large
	$ per unit	$ per unit	$ per unit
Original cost	10	15	20
Estimated selling price	14	18	19
Selling and distribution costs	1	4	3
	Units	Units	Units
Units in inventories	300	400	600

The value of inventories at the year-end should be:

$ _____

18 An organisation's cash book has an opening balance in the bank column of $900 credit. 'The following transactions then took place:

• cash sales $2,300 including sales tax of $300;

• receipts from customers of $7,200;

• payments to payables of $5,000 less 5% cash discount;

• dishonoured cheques from customers amounting to $400.

The closing balance in the bank column of the cash book should be:

$ _____

CONTROLLING THE BOOKKEEPING SYSTEM

SYNOPSIS

Bank Reconciliations

The balance on a bank statement may not equal the balance in the cash book.

This may occur where there are permanent differences or errors on either the bank statement or the cash book, and the bank statement or the cash book will need to be amended

For example:

- bank charges not entered in the cash book
- incorrect direct debit on a bank statement

The difference between bank statement and cash book may be due to timing differences – that is, they will become equal in time but at a point in time they are not equal.

For example:

- Cheques paid out which have been entered in the cash book but which have not yet been presented at the bank.
- Cheques received which have been entered in the cash book but which have not yet been cleared by the bank.

A bank reconciliation is prepared to reconcile (i.e. explain) the difference between a bank statement and cash book.

Supplier Statement Reconciliations

This is similar to a bank statement reconciliation. The balance on a supplier's statement may not equal the balance in the purchase ledger.

This may occur where there are permanent differences or errors on either the supplier's statement or the purchase ledger, and the supplier's statement or the purchase ledger will need to be amended.

For example:

- Invoice from supplier posted to the wrong purchase ledger account
- Supplier's statement includes an invoice for goods which were never ordered

The difference between supplier's statement and purchase ledger may be due to timing differences – that is, they will become equal in time but at a point in time they are not equal.

For example:

- Cheque recently sent to supplier which the supplier has not yet entered in his sales ledger.
- Invoice sent by supplier entered in the purchase day book but not yet posted to the supplier's purchase ledger account.

A supplier's statement reconciliation is prepared to reconcile (i.e. explain) the difference between a supplier's statement and a purchase ledger balance.

Control accounts

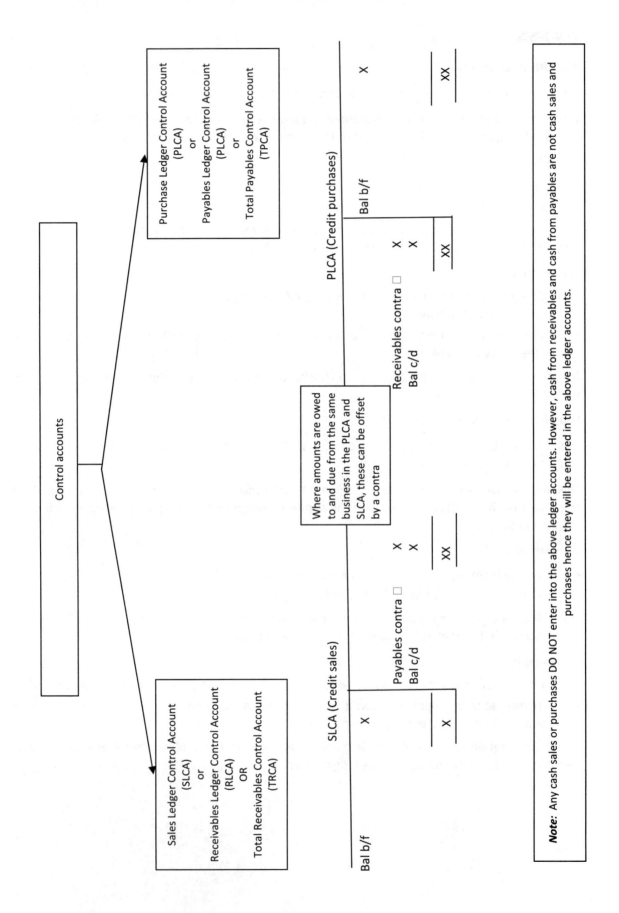

SLCA

Debit		Credit		
Bal b/f	X	Return inwards	X	→ Debit returns inwards to decrease sales (which are credit balances in the I/S)
Sales as per sales day book	X	Bad debts	X	→ Bad debt is an expense which are debit hence control account is a credit
Sales tax on sales	X	Cash from receivables	X	→ Cash received from receivables will be debit bank hence credit control account
Dishonoured cheques	X	Discount allowed	X	→ Expense to company hence debit, therefore opposite in control account – credit
Bad debts written back	X	Payables contra	X	→ PLCA will be a debit, so credit in SLCA
Bal c/d	X	Bal c/d	X	
	XX		XX	

Sales as per sales day book → Sales are credit, hence debit control account

Dishonoured cheques → Cheque that has been returned by the bank hence we will need to credit the bank a/c and debit control account

Dishonoured cheques

Reasons are as follows:

(i) Insufficient funds
(ii) State cheques (out of date) – more than 6 months old
(iii) Words and figures (amount are different)
(iv) Wrong signatures or not enough signatures
(v) Stopped cheque
(vi) 'Postdated cheque' → date can be made in a month's time

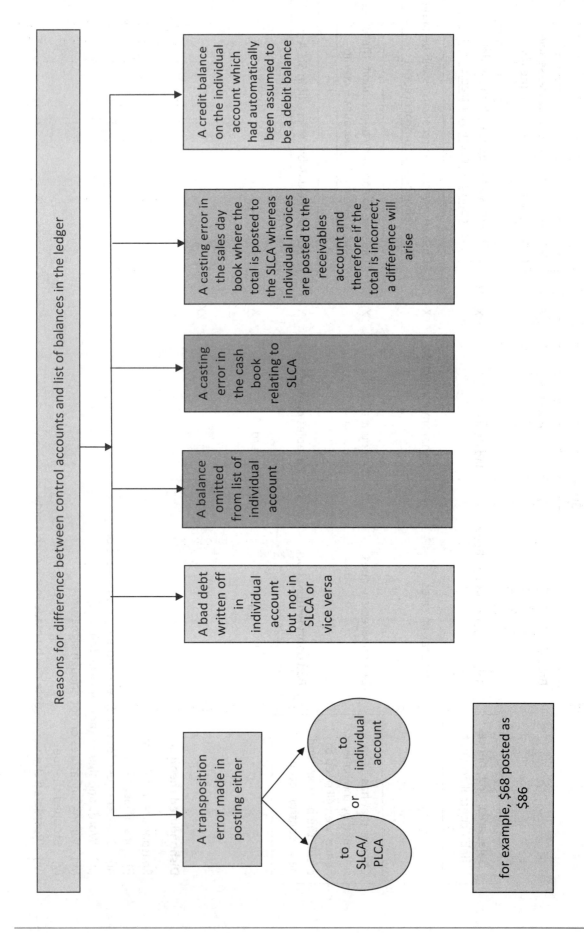

Suspense Accounts

A trial balance may not agree where there is an error in the accounting books. A suspense account is opened for the difference in the trial balance. For example, if the debit side is greater than the credit side by $1,000, then a suspense account will have to be opened with a credit balance of $1,000 to make the totals in the trial balance agree.

This balance will remain on the suspense account until the error(s) are discovered. Note that, in the example above, if there is a credit balance on the suspense account, then when the error is discovered, the double entry will involve a debit to the suspense account, in order to eliminate the suspense account balance.

Similarly, if there is a debit balance on the suspense account, then when the error is discovered, the double entry will involve a credit to the suspense account, in order to eliminate the suspense account balance.

You should be able to work out the effect of errors on the trial balance.

For example, if there is a credit balance on the suspense account, the error could be:

Omitted sales

Overstated purchases

Omitted liability

Overstated asset, e.g. receivables

For example, if there is a debit balance on the suspense account, the error could be:

Omitted expense

Overstated revenue

Omitted asset, e.g. prepayment

Overstated liability, e.g. payable

19 From the following information, calculate the value of purchases:

	$
Opening payables	71,300
Cash paid	271,150
Discounts received	6,600
Goods returned	13,750
Closing payables	68,900

20 A suspense account shows a credit balance of $260. This could be due to

A   omitting a sale of $260 from the sales ledger

B   recording a purchase of $260 twice in the purchases account

C   failing to write off a bad debt of $260

D   recording an electricity bill paid of $130 by debiting the bank account and crediting the electricity account

21   You are given the following information:

	$
Receivables at 1 January 2003	30,000
Receivables at 31 December 2003	27,000
Total receipts during 2003 (including cash sales of $15,000)	255,000

Sales on credit during 2003 amount to

THE REGULATORY FRAMEWORK OF ACCOUNTING

SYNOPSIS

There are four separate but related bodies which control the setting of International Financial Reporting Standards (IFRS). They are organised as in the figure below.

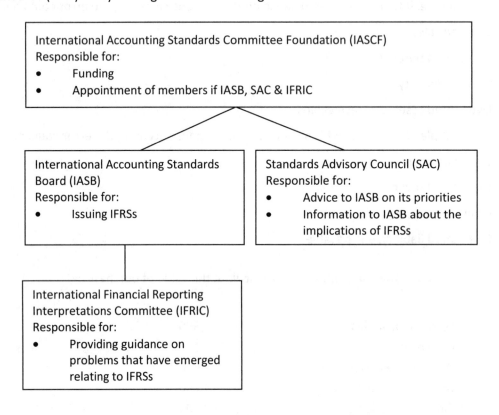

Members of these bodies are drawn from preparers of financial statements, (accountants) and users of financial statements (banks, analysts, stock exchange, government, etc.), all from different parts of the world.

The IASB sets IFRSs; a previous body, known as the International Accounting Standards Committee (IASC) sets International Accounting Standards (IAS). When the IASB came into existence it adopted all of the IAS, issued by the IASC. Thus we have in existence two sets of standards – IFRS and IAS, with the IAS being the older standards. In general, when reference is made to IFRS, it includes the IASs.

QUALITATIVE CHARACTERISTICS OF FINANCIAL STATEMENTS

- relevant
- reliable
- complete
- comparable
- understandable
- timely

ACCOUNTING CONVENTIONS

- *Going concern.* Financial statements are prepared on the basis that the business is to continue for the foreseeable future.
- *Consistency.* The accounting treatment of like items is consistently applied from one period to the next.
- *Accruals and matching.* Revenues and expenses are recognised as they are earned or incurred (irrespective of whether or not they are paid for), and matched with each other, in that the revenue from a transaction is matched with the expense incurred in producing that revenue.
- *Prudence.* A business should not claim to have made profits or gains before they have been earned with reasonable certainty, but should anticipate fully any losses that are expected to occur. This prevents overstating of assets or profits.
- *Realisation.* Revenue and profits should not be anticipated but should be recognised in financial statements when they are realised in the form of cash, or other asset, which can be converted into cash.
- *Business entity.* This convention separates the individual(s) behind a business from the business itself, and only records transactions in the accounts that affect the business.
- *Money measurement.* This limits the recognition of accounting events to those that can be expressed in money terms.
- *Historical cost.* The historical cost of an asset is the original amount paid for an asset when it was acquired.
- *Objectivity.* Financial statements should not be influenced by the personal bias of the person preparing them.
- *Dual aspect.* This convention is the basis of double-entry bookkeeping and it means that every transaction entered into has a double effect on the position of the entity as recorded in the ledger accounts at the time of that transaction.
- *Periodicity.* It is necessary to assess the assets and liabilities (i.e., statement of financial position) and performance (i.e. income statement) of an organisation by producing periodic financial statements.
- *Materiality.* This ensures that the information provided to users is clear by omitting items that are not significant to the user in understanding the overall financial position of the organisation.
- *Stable monetary unit.* It is assumed that the monetary value of a currency is stable from one period to the next.

INCOMPLETE RECORDS AND INCOME AND EXPENDITURE STATEMENTS

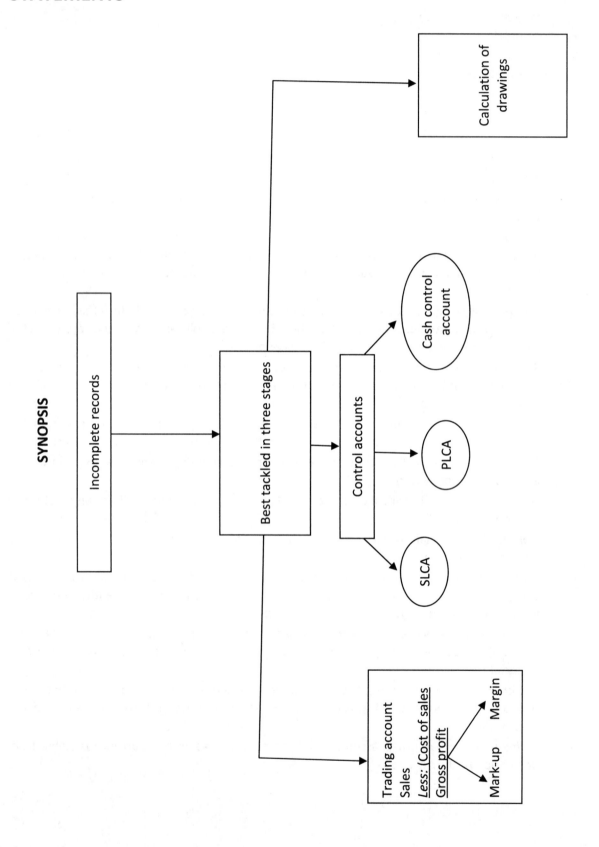

INCOMPLETE RECORDS

Reasons:

(a)   Owner of the business does not keep proper accounting records.

(b)   Natural disasters, earthquake, fire, flood and so on.

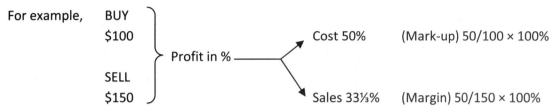

For example,   BUY
                 $100
                            Profit in % ———— Cost 50%   (Mark-up) 50/100 × 100%

                 SELL
                 $150   Sales 33⅓%   (Margin) 50/150 × 100%

Calculate the cost of goods which have been sold for $1,200 on which a mark-up on cost of sales of 25% has been achieved.

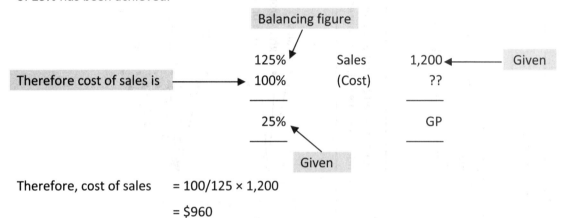

	Balancing figure		
	125%	Sales	1,200 ← Given
Therefore cost of sales is →	100%	(Cost)	??
	25%		GP
	Given		

Therefore, cost of sales   = 100/125 × 1,200

                             = $960

Trading discount – Mark-up/Margin

For example, if I buy an item for $100
and sell it for $150 then my profit is $50.
In terms of % it will be either

50% → Mark-up → Profit/cost × 100% = 50/100 × 100 = 50%

or → Why?

33⅓% → Margin → Profit/sales × 100% = 50/150 × 100 = 33⅓%

As a result of this, students often get confused when it comes to dealing with profit that is based on cost and that based on selling price. Therefore, you must read the exam questions careful and the best way to take this problem is to understand the following concept.

%

Sales
• Sales
• gross profit on sales
• gross profit margin
• margin

becomes 100% if examiner uses the following terminology for percentage based on

cost
• cost
• cost of sales
• gross profit on cost
• gross profit on cost of sales
• gross profit on mark-up
• mark-up

becomes 100% if examiner uses the following terminology for percentage based on

100% Sales

100% (Cost of sales)

Given % Gross profit } Margin

Mark-up

% will normally be given in exam question

INCOMPLETE RECORDS AND CONTROL ACCOUNTS

Whenever the examiners use the following words or terminology, always consider opening a SLCA to calculate the sales figure.

(i)   Opening receivables

(ii)   Closing receivables

(iii)   Amount received from receivables

SLCA

	$		$
Opening bal b/f	X	Amount received from receivables	X
Balancing figure sales	X	Closing bal c/d	X
	——		——
	XX		XX
	——		——

Whenever the examiner uses the following words or terminology, always consider opening a PLCA to calculate the purchase figure.

(i)   Opening payables

(ii)   Closing payables

(iii)   Cash/cheque paid to payables

PLCA

	$		$
Cash paid to payables	X	Opening bal b/f	X
Closing bal c/d	X	Balancing figure purchases	X
	——		——
	XX		XX
	——		——

Wherever the examiner uses the following words, then consider trading account.

(i)   Opening inventories (if first year of trading, this will not be given)

(ii)   Closing inventories

	$	$
Sales *(from SLCA if not given)*		X
Opening inventories	X	
Add: Purchases *(from PLCA if not given)*	X	
	——	
	X	
	——	
Less: Closing inventories	(X)	
Cost of goods sold		(X)
		——
Gross profit		X
		——

INCOME AND EXPENDITURE STATEMENTS

Clubs and societies are not-for-profit organisations and often one of the members may be the treasurer. Such treasurers may be inexperienced and will often just keep a very simply cashbook; in rare cases, the books may be incomplete, and hence this topic is combined with that of incomplete records. The techniques described above for incomplete records will therefore apply to clubs and societies.

The financial statements of not-for-profit organisations will differ from commercial businesses:

- *Income and expenditure account,* not income statement
- *Surplus /deficit,* not profit/loss
- *Accumulated fund*, not capital
- Separate trading accounts for bar and social events
- Treatment of membership fees:
    - Life membership – spread over a period of years – life membership fund in statement of financial position
    - Joining fees – spread over a period of years – joining fees fund in statement of financial position
    - Membership fees in arrears – usually ignored – no receivables
    - Membership fees in advance – deferred revenue – current liability
- Depreciation – may use 'revaluation method' for sundry small items of equipment

22 Mark-up on cost of sales = 10%

Sales $6,160

Cost of sales ????

23 Gross profit on sales = 20%

Cost of sales $20,000

Sales ????

24 Mark-up on cost of sales = 33⅓%

Cost of sales $15,000

Sales ?????

25 Sales $20,000

Cost of sales $16,000

What is

(a) the margin, and

(b) the mark-up?

26 Pritesh started business on 1 January 2005. The following relates to year ended 31 December 2005.

	$
Trade payables at 31 December 2005	16,000
Trade receivables at 31 December 2005	12,000
Cash received from receivables	32,000
Cash paid to payables	28,000
Mark-up on cost	30%

Calculate the closing inventories at 31 December 2005.

27 Devan had the following transactions relating to his business.

	$
Cash received from receivables	18,500
Due from receivables 1/1/2004	1,000
Opening inventories	2,000
Closing inventories	500
Due to suppliers 1/1/2004	750
Due to suppliers 31/12/2004	300
Cash paid to suppliers	1,200

Calculate:

(i) Sales

A	$19,500	C	$18,500
B	$17,500	D	None of the above

(ii) Purchases

A	$2,250	C	$150
B	$750	D	None of the above

(iii) Gross profit

A	$15,250	C	$16,250
B	$750	D	$18,250

(iv) Gross profit as % of sales

A	92%	C	82%
B	93%	D	87%

(v) Gross profit as % of cost

A	678%	C	114%
B	14%	D	87%

THE MANUFACTURING ACCOUNT

SYNOPSIS

So far we have worked with trading accounts of the form:

	$	
Sales		X
Opening inventories	X	
Add: Purchases	X	
	———	
	X	
Less: Closing inventories	(X)	
	———	
Cost of sales		(X)
		———
Gross profit		X
		———

This is perfectly satisfactory for a retail organisation that purchases and resells goods. A manufacturing company will need further details for the cost of manufacturing its products and these details can be set out in the form of manufacturing account.

DEFINITIONS

- *Direct costs* are those which can be attributed to a particular unit of production and will normally include raw materials, productive wages and other expenses capable of direct identification with production. These three are often called direct materials, direct wages and direct expenses.
- *Indirect expenses* are production expenses which cannot be attributed to a particular unit of production. They are often called manufacturing or works overheads and will include such items as factory power, plant repairs and so on.
- *Prime cost* is the total of direct expenses.
- *Factory cost* or works cost is prime cost plus factory indirect expenses.

INVENTORIES

A trading firm has inventories in only one form (i.e., goods held for resale), but a manufacturing firm will have three forms of inventories:

1   Raw materials – items of raw materials which have not yet been issued to production;

2   Work-in-progress – items of partly completed goods;

3   Finished goods – items which are completed but unsold.

THE PRO FORMA

Basic format

The manufacturing account summarises the costs of production in the factory:

	$
Direct materials	X
Direct labour	X
Direct expenses	X
	―――
Prime cost	X
Manufacturing overheads	X
	―――
Factory cost	X
	―――

Pro forma manufacturing account

	$	$
Materials consumed		
Opening inventories of raw materials	X	
Add: Purchases of raw materials	X	
	―――	
	X	
Less: Closing inventories of raw materials	(X)	
	―――	X
Direct wages		X
Direct expenses		X
		―――
Prime cost		X
Works indirect expenses		
Factory power	X	
Factory rent	X	
Factory insurance	X	
Factory light and heat	X	
Plant repairs	X	
Plant depreciation	X	
	―――	X
Add: Opening work-in-progress		X
Less: Closing work-in-progress		(X)
		―――
Factory cost of goods produced – transfers to warehouse		X
		―――

INCOME STATEMENT

The income statement, which takes account of selling and distribution expenses and administration expenses, will be in a reasonably familiar format:

Income statement

	$	$
Sales		X
Less: Cost of goods sold		
Opening inventories of finished goods	X	
Add: Transfers from warehouse	X	
	X	
Less: Closing inventories of finished goods	(X)	
		(X)
Gross profit		X
Less: Distribution expenses	X	
Administrative expenses	X	
		(X)
Net profit		X

28 There is only one large question in this section. This question would not be typical of a question in the computer-based assessment (CBA), which would only deal with one small aspect of this larger question. However, it allows you the opportunity to put together much of what you have learnt in previous chapters as well as the current chapter on manufacturing accounts.

The balances extracted from the nominal ledger of Drogba at 31 July 20X1 were as follows:

	$
Inventory of raw materials at 1 August 20X0	4,000
Work in progress at 1 August 20X0	2,000
Inventory of finished goods at 1 August 20X0	8,000
Direct factory wages	60,000
Office salaries	50,000
Drawings by Drogba	40,000
Purchases of raw materials	90,000
Depreciation charge on factory machinery	35,000
Depreciation charge on office machinery	15,000
Factory overheads	35,000
Advertising	18,000
Sales	450,000
Factory machinery	400,000
Office machinery	200,000
Accumulated depreciation on factory machinery at 31 July 20X1	90,000
Accumulated depreciation on office machinery at 31 July 20X1	30,000
Receivables	40,000
Payables	7,000
Bank overdraft	3,000
Bank loan	80,000
Capital at 1 August 20X0	337,000

The valuation of inventories at 31 July 20X1 was as follows:

Raw materials	$3,000
Work in progress	$1,500
Finished goods	$6,000

Prepare an income statement, including a manufacturing account, for the year ended 31 July 20X1 and a statement of financial position at that date.

THE FINANCIAL STATEMENTS OF LIMITED COMPANIES AND STATEMENT OF CASH FLOWS

Note – students taking the computer based assessment before May 2010 should see the author's note on page xi in the chapter Computer Based Assessment; Syllabus regarding the revised IAS 1 Presentation of Financial Statements

SYNOPSIS

EXAMPLES OF THE LAYOUT OF FINANCIAL STATEMENTS OF LIMITED COMPANIES

Statement of Comprehensive Income (when produced as a single statement)

Statement of Comprehensive Income for the year ended (date)

Revenue (Working 1)	A	X
Cost of sales (Working 2)	B	(X)
Gross profit/(loss)		X
Other operating income	C	X
Selling and distribution expense	D	(X)
Administration expense	E	(X)
Operating profit		X
Interest received		X
Interest paid	F	(X)
Profit before tax		X
Income tax		(X)
Profit for the period		X
Other comprehensive income		
Gain on property revaluation before tax	X	
Income tax	(X)	
Gain on property revaluation after tax		X
Total comprehensive income for the year		X

Working 1

Revenue:	Made up of	Sales		X
		– Sales return		(X)
		– Sales tax		(X)
		Revenue	A	X

Working 2

Cost of sales:	Made up of	Opening inventories		X
		+ Purchases	X	
		+ Carriage inwards	X	
		– Returns outwards	(X)	
		– Sales tax on purchases	(X)	
				X
				X
		Closing inventories		(X)
		Cost of sales	B	X

Other operating income
Includes the following:

(i)	Rent received		X
(ii)	Commission received		X
(iii)	Discount received		X
(iv)	Profit on disposal of non-current assets		X
		C	X

Selling and distribution expenses

Warehouse rent	X	
Carriage outwards	X	
Sales director's salary	X	
Depreciation of car (sales staff)	X	
Administration expenses for distribution	X	
Depreciation of delivery van	X	
Depreciation of sales directors' car	X	
Advertising	X	
	D	X

Administration expenses

Light and heat of admin. office	X	
Rent of admin. building	X	
Wages staff in administration	X	
Depreciation of car (admin. staff)	X	
	E	X

If in doubt and not sure whether an expense is 'selling and distribution 'or administration; assume it is an administration expense

Interest payable and similar charges

This expense must be shown separately. It includes the following:

(i)	Interest on loans		X
(ii)	Interest on overdraft		X
(iii)	Bank charges		X
			___
		F	X
			___

Income tax

The figure for income tax will normally be given to you. Sometimes you may be asked to take a percentage of the profit. In either case, you will accrue the income tax in the statement of comprehensive income and include in current liabilities in the statement of financial position. The accrual for tax is treated in the same way as any other accrual, and is reversed in the next year. The accrual for income tax has to be agreed with the tax authorities and where there is a disagreement this may result in there having been an under or over accrual for tax. Under accruals are added to the income tax charge in the following year, and vice versa for over accruals.

Note that in a sole trader's business, tax is a personal charge, and so does not appear in the financial statements.

Companies may choose to produce a single statement of comprehensive income, as illustrated above, or to produce two statements – an income statement and a modified statement of comprehensive income.

The income statement would be the lines 'Revenue' down to and including 'Profit for the period'.

The modified statement of comprehensive income would then begin with and repeat 'Profit for the period' and then show other comprehensive income.

Statement of Comprehensive Income

(when produced as a second statement, rather than a single statement, after an income statement)

Profit for the period		X
Other comprehensive income		
Gain on property revaluation before tax	X	
Income tax	(X)	
	___	
Gain on property revaluation after tax		X
		___
Total comprehensive income for the year		X
		___

The tax will be included as an accrual under non-current liabilities in the statement of financial position.

The total comprehensive income for the year will be shown in the statement of changes in equity, analysed between profit for the period and the net gain after tax on property revaluation.

In the CBA the question should make it clear what type of format is required. In general, an income statement will be required where there is no revaluation of property. Where there is a revaluation, a single statement of comprehensive income will normally be required. However, students should be aware that there is an option to produce two separate statements, as explained above. On some occasions, a question may ask for just 'other comprehensive income', and this will be an extract from the statement of comprehensive income, as illustrated above.

In this Exam Practice Kit, the statement will be referred to as a 'statement of comprehensive income' regardless of whether there is an 'other comprehensive income' section. This assumes that a company is using the single statement format.

The Statement of Changes in Equity (SCE)

Statement of changes in equity for the year ended (date)

	Ordinary shares	Share premium	Revaluation reserve	General reserve	Retained earnings	Total
Balance 1 Jan X6	X	X	X		X	X
Profit after tax					X	X
Dividends					(X)	(X)
Revaluation			X			X
Shares issued	X	X				X
Transfer				X	(X)	
Balance 31 Dec X6	X	X	X	X	X	X

The SCE shows the change in equity over the year, where equity is the share capital plus reserves in a company. The SCE shows the transactions between a company and it owners, and these transactions include:

- Total comprehensive income
- Dividends
- Issue of shares, which may be at a premium

There may a transfer between reserves, for example from retained earnings to the general reserve; this will change those individual reserves but not the total of equity.

The CBA may require you to prepare a SCE, but not all the columns will be required if there has been no change – for example, if shares have not been issued. Again for simplification, the total column may not be required.

Dividends

Dividends often paid in two instalments: interim dividend during the year; final dividend after the year end. The total of the dividends appears in the SCE.

Final dividends. Directors propose a final dividend which, when approved at the AGM after the year end, becomes a declared dividend. Final dividends are recognised only when the dividend has been declared.

This means that in most circumstances the dividends which are paid in a year are the final dividend of the previous year and the interim dividend of the current year.

Directors do not have to pay dividends in two instalments and where there is only one dividend, this is dealt with in the same way as a final dividend.

There may be some occasions where the directors declare a final dividend before the end of the year, but do not pay the dividend until after the year end. In this situation, the accruals convention is applied and the declared dividend will appear in the statement of changes in equity, and there will also be a 'dividend liability' in the current liabilities in the statement of financial position.

Preference share dividends are complex and any CBA question should make clear how any dividend is to be dealt with.

Types of shares

General differences	Preference shares	Ordinary shares
Amount of Dividends	Fixed %	Fluctuate
Liquidation	Paid first	Paid last
Dividends	Must pay	Not necessary to pay
Owner	Investors	Owners
Vote	No Votes	Voting rights

Statement of Financial Position

Statement of Financial Position at (date)

	Cost	Accumulated depreciation	Carrying amount
	$	$	$
ASSETS			
Non-current assets			
Land and buildings	X	(X)	X
Plant and machinery	X	(X)	X
Motor van	X	(X)	X
Fixtures and fittings	X	(X)	X
	X	(X)	x
Current assets			
Inventories		X	
Receivables		X	
Current investments		X	
Prepayments		X	
Bank		X	
Cash		X	
			X
			X

Equity and liabilities

Share capital		X
Share premium		X
Revaluation reserve		X
Retained earnings		X
General reserves		X
		———
		X

Non-current liabilities

Loans	X	
Income tax on gains	X	
Debentures	X	
	———	X

Current liabilities

Overdraft	X	
Trade payables	X	
Accruals	X	
Income tax	X	
Dividends – declared	X	
	———	X
		———
		X
		———

Liabilities

Liabilities due in less than 1 year are current liabilities, e.g. bank overdraft

Liabilities due in more than 1 year are non-current liabilities, e.g. 5 year bank loan.

Bottom half of statement of financial position for:

(a)		(b)	
Sole trader		Ltd company	
Capital	X	Share capital	X
Net profit	X	Retained earnings	X
– Drawings	(X)	Reserves	X
	——		——
	X		X
	——		——

In limited company financial statements, there are no drawings, these are replaced by dividends and shown in the SCE.

Share capital

Authorised share capital:

These are the maximum number of shares that a company is allowed to issue. Such type of shares will NEVER effect the calculations within the financial statements. If given in the exam question, then you will simply ignore it.

Issued share capital:

These are the number of shares that a company issues. Such shares will affect the calculations within the financial statements. Every share when first issued has a nominal value (NV) or face value or par value. Normally, shares are issued at nominal value of $1. If so, then the calculations of dividends is straightforward and simple. However, if nominal value is 0.50c, 0.75c or 0.25c, then you must think carefully when calculating the dividend figure.

For example,

Company issues 10,000 $1 ordinary shares

Mr X buys 75%

Mrs Y buys 25%

Dr Bank $10,000

Cr Share capital $10,000

If the share price fluctuate (increase/decrease) in the market, then the share capital is never effected. It is the individual shareholders that will benefit or lose on such situations.

Share premium A/C:

This arises when shares are issued at greater than nominal value.

Fluctuation within the market will not affect the share premium account.

For example, a company issues 10,000 $1 ordinary shares @ $1.60

Dr Bank	$16,000	
Cr Share capital		$10,000
Cr Share premium		$6,000

A company issues $10,000 $1 ordinary shares and declares a dividend of 10c/share: 10,000 = shares @ 10c = $1000.

Note: Always convert dollar into shares.

Company issues $10,000 50c ordinary shares and declares a dividend of 10c/share.

Convert the $ = shares

$10,000 divided into 50c shares = 20,000 shares

Shares	20,000
	× 0.10
	———
Dividends	2,000
	———

FORMAT OF THE STATEMENT OF CASH FLOWS

International Accounting Standard (IAS 7) deals with the statement of cash flows. This was previously called a cash flow statement. It prescribes the following format:

Pro forma per IAS 7

Statement of cash flows for the year ended 31 March 20X2

	$	$
Cash flows from operating activities		
Operating profit		X
Adjustments for		
Depreciation		X
(Profit)/Loss on sale of non-current assets		(X)/X
Working capital adjustments		
(Increase)/decrease in receivables		(X)/X
Increase/(decrease) in payables		X/(X)
(Increase)/decrease in inventories		(X)/X
Cash generated from operations		X
(Interest paid)		(X)
(Tax paid)		(X)
		—
		X
Cash flows from investing activities		
(Purchase of non-current assets)	(X)	
Proceeds on sale of non-current assets	X	
Interest received	X	
Dividends received	X	
	—	X

Cash flows from financing activities

Proceeds from issue of shares	X	
Proceeds from loans	X	
(Repayment of loans)	(X)	
(Payment of dividends)	(X)	
	——	X
		——
Net increase in bank and cash		X
Bank and cash at the beginning of the period		X
		——
Bank and cash at the end of the period		X
		——

Note that the brackets in the above pro forma show whether the cash flow is positive or (negative).

Statement of cash flows Points to consider

- Always think cash only when dealing with this topic.
- Always think cash inflow (+) and cash outflow (—) (If cash outflow, do not forget brackets.).
- There are no accruals effects in this topic; in other words everything is cash.
- Depreciation will always be a positive – depreciation does not involve cash.
- Profit or loss on sale of non-current assets is removed from the 'operating activities' section because the profit/loss is not a cash flow. Loss on sale of non-current assets will be positive; vice versa, a profit will be negative. The cash flow from the sale of non-current assets is recorded in the 'investing activities' section.
- Watch out for the positive and negative cash flow in the working capital; an increase in a liability is positive; an increase in an asset is negative; and vice versa. Practice reciting the effects of all possible changes in working capital.

	Increase	*Decrease*
Assets		
Inventories	Negative	Positive
Receivables	Negative	Positive
Prepayments	Negative	Positive
Liabilities		
Payables	Positive	Negative
Accruals	Positive	Negative

- Taxation

  This will be the tax that the company may have paid during the year – negative (don't forget the brackets). Any repayments of tax will be positive.
- Dividends paid

  The payment will always be negative. Do not forget brackets.
- One would normally expect a statement of comprehensive income to be before the statement of financial position. However, in the CBA, watch out as the examiner tends to show the statement of financial position before the statement of comprehensive income.
- Always circle the years within the question. Watch the order in which the columns are presented; the most recent year is usually the first column, but sometimes in the CBA the first column may be the earlier year.

  Preparation of the statement of cash flows

  The practical preparation of a statement of cash flows is looked at in the question 30 below.

29   The trial balance of Maci plc at the year ended 31 December 20X1 was as follows:

	$000	$000
Premises – at valuation	750	
Accumulated depreciation on premises		120
Inventories at 1 January 20X1	60	
Receivables	110	
Payables		25
Patent – at cost	100	
Bank		30
Sales		1,500
Purchases	250	
10% Debentures		100
Debenture interest	5	
Interim dividend	10	
Directors' remuneration	40	
Administration expenses	380	
Selling and distribution expenses	325	
Deprecation charge	20	
Ordinary shares of $1		200
Retained earnings at 1 January 20X1		50
General reserve		25
	2,050	2,050

Schedule of adjustments:

(i)   Inventories at 31 December 20X1 was valued at $70,000

(ii)   The debenture interest should be accrued

(iii)   The directors declare a final dividend of $12,000

(iv)   In September 20X1 $30,000 taxation was paid, which was the amount owing for the year ended 31 December 20X0. The tax advisers estimate that the taxation for the year ended 31 December 20X1 will be $10,000, but the tax computation has not yet been submitted to the tax authorities.

(v)   The directors decide to transfer $15,000 to the general reserve.

(vi)   The property is to be revalued to $825,000, with potential tax on the gain of $20,000.

Complete the missing figures and words in the financial statements set out below.

Maci plc Statement of comprehensive income

		$000
Sales		1,500
Opening inventories Purchases	250	
Purchases		
Closing inventories		
	_____	
Cost of sales		
		_____
Gross profit		
Administration expenses	380	
Selling and distribution expenses	325	
Depreciation charge	20	
Directors' remuneration	40	
	_____	
		_____
Operating profit		
Debenture interest		
		_____
Profit before tax		
Taxation		
		_____
Profit after tax		
Other operating income		
Gain on property revaluation		
Income tax		
	_____	
Net gain on property revaluation		
		_____
Total comprehensive income		
		_____

Maci plc

Statement of change in equity for the year ended 31 December 20X1

	Share Capital	Revaluation reserve	Retained earnings	General reserve	Total
	$000	$000	$000	$000	$000
Bal b/f					
	_____	_____	_____	_____	_____
Bal c/f					
	_____	_____	_____	_____	_____

Maci plc

Statement of Financial Position at 31 December 20X1

	$000	$000	$000
ASSETS	Cost	Depreciation	
Non-current assets			
Patent			
Premises	___	___	___
	___	___	
Current Assets			
Inventories			
Receivables	___		
			___
			___
EQUITY AND LIABILITIES			
Ordinary shares of $1			
Revaluation reserve			
General reserve			
Retained earnings at 31 December 20X1			___
Non-current liabilities			
Debentures			
Income tax on gain		___	
Current liabilities			
Bank			
Payables			
		___	___
			___

30 The draft financial statements of Seafield Ltd for the year ended 30 April 20X5 are set out below:

Seafield Ltd

Statement of financial position as at 30 April 20X5

	20X5 $000	20X4 $000
Non-current assets (Note 1)	1,473	1,929
Current assets		
Inventories	2,679	2,064
Trade receivables	2,379	1,818
Cash at bank and in hand	9	30
	5,067	3,912
	6,540	5,841

Equity and liabilities

Share capital	2,460	2,154
Retained earnings	765	213
	3,225	2,367

Non-current liabilities

Loans	1,248	1,665

Current liabilities

Trade payables	1,749	1,689
Dividends declared	198	114
Taxation	120	6
	2,067	1,809
	6,540	5,841

Seafield Ltd

Statement of comprehensive income for the year ended 30 April 20X5

	20X5		20X4	
	$000	$000	$000	$000
Revenue		8,790		4,689
Directors' emoluments	210		210	
Auditors' remuneration	18		15	
Depreciation	18		15	
Profit on sale of non-current assets	(615)			
Other operating expenses	8,172		4,293	
		(7,803)		(4,533)
Operating profit		987		156
Interest on loans		(117)		(138)
Profit before tax		870		18
Income tax		(120)		(6)
Profit for the period		750		12

Seafield Ltd

Statement of changes in equity for the year ended 30 April 20X5

	$000
Balance as at 1 May 20X4	213
Profit for the period	750
Dividends declared (Note 2)	(198)
Balance as at 30 April 20X5	765

Note1

	Land	Plant	Total
Cost 1/5/X4	1,365	849	2,214
Addition	–	159	159
Disposal	(345)	(327)	(672)
Cost 30/4/X5	1,020	681	1,701
Cumulative depn 1/5/X4	–	285	285
Depreciation charge	–	18	18
Disposal	–	(75)	(75)
Cumulative depn 30/4/X5	–	228	228
Carrying amount 30/4/X5	1,020	453	1,473
Carrying amount 1/5/X4	1,365	564	1,929

Note 2

1   The directors declared a dividend, which was approved by the shareholders, of $114,000 on the 1 April 20X4 which was paid on the 1 June 20X4.

2   The directors declared a dividend, which was approved by the shareholders, of $198,000 on the 1 April 20X5 which was paid on the 1 June 20X5.

Requirement:

Prepare a statement of cash flows for Seafield Ltd for the year ended 30 April 20X5

THE INTERPRETATION OF FINANCIAL STATEMENTS

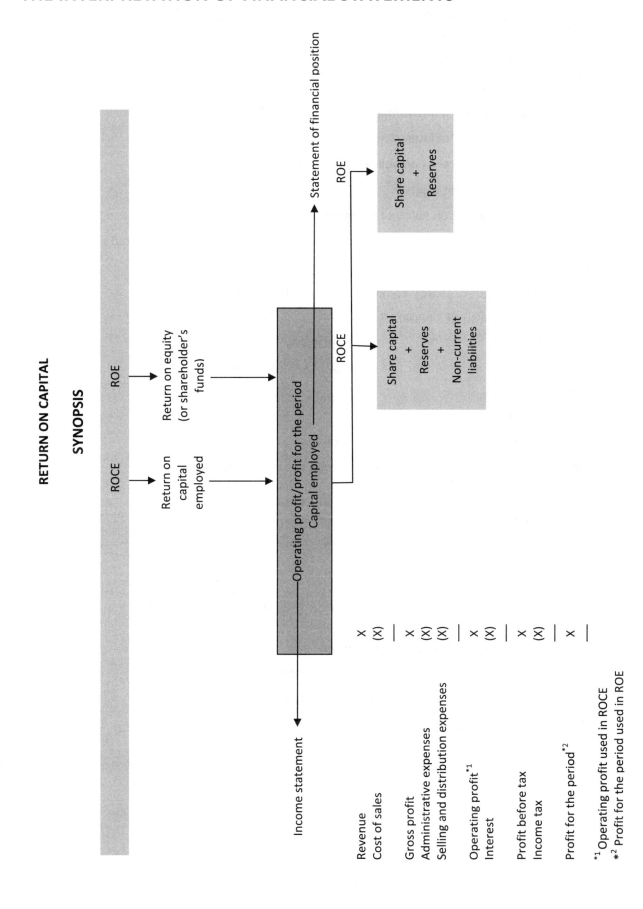

RETURN ON CAPITAL

SYNOPSIS

In summary:

$$ROCE = \frac{\text{Operating profit}}{\text{Equity} + \text{Long term liabilitie s}}$$

$$ROE = \frac{\text{Profit for the period}}{\text{Equity}}$$

Factors to consider when answering question on ROCE/ROE

1   Consider the rate of interest

2   Consider the depreciation policies of the company

3   Age of non-current assets

4   Consider revaluation policy of the company

5   Consider intangible assets within the company, like trademark, royalties and goodwill

6   Consider position of non-current liabilities

7   Consider issue of shares: company is going to lose control.

GROSS PROFIT % AND NET PROFIT %

GROSS PROFIT %	**NET PROFIT %**
$\dfrac{GP}{\text{Sales}} \times 100 = a\%$	$\dfrac{\text{Net profit or profit for the period}}{\text{Sales}} \times 100 = b\%$

Say gross profit is 20%

At $100 sales you made $20 profit before expenses

When can gross profit percentage go down even though revenue increases.

For example

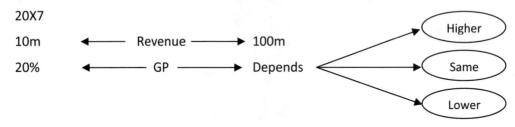

    20X7

    10m   ←——— Revenue ———→ 100m

    20%   ←——— GP ———→ Depends

    Higher / Same / Lower

1   Selling goods on special offer at reduced selling price

2   Cost of goods increased but selling price remained the same

3   Consider pilferage, damaged goods, obsolete goods

4   Sales mix, that is the company starts selling different products, with lower profit margin.

LIQUIDITY RATIOS

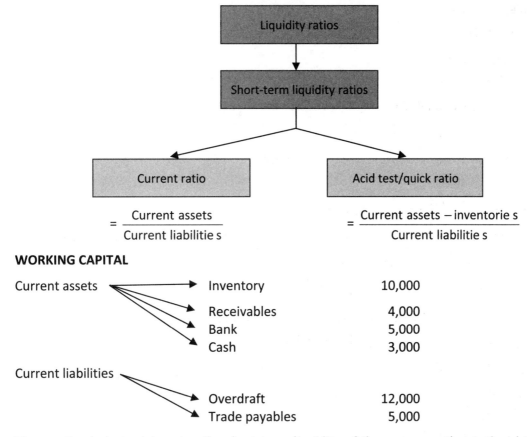

WORKING CAPITAL

Current assets	Inventory	10,000
	Receivables	4,000
	Bank	5,000
	Cash	3,000
Current liabilities	Overdraft	12,000
	Trade payables	5,000

These ratios help to determine the short-term liquidity of the company, that is the ability of the company to pay its debts as and when they fall due. Both these ratios must be calculated together. If the answer is 1:1, then the current assets equal the current liabilities. In the example above, the company has approximately 29% more current assets to pay off the current liabilities.

$$\frac{CA}{CC} = \frac{22,000}{17,000} = 1.29 : 1$$

Any perceived surplus of net current assets could be invested in order to earn interest or even used to reduce the overdraft facility.

Cash at bank $5,000. If the bank balance is more than the business needs to manage its cash flow, then any surplus should be invested.

Receivables $5,000. If receivables are excessive, then:

1   Credit control position needs to be reviewed.

2   Risk of bad debts increases.

3   Money tied up unnecessarily.

Receivables days = average receivables/credit sales x 365

This ratio helps determine the number of days that is taken by the customers to pay us.

Inventory turnover ratio = $\dfrac{\text{Cost of sales}}{\text{Inventories}}$ = No. of times

Average inventories — (Opening inventory + Closing inventory) /2

For example,

20X7	20X8
6 times	10 times

Convert the answer in no. of

Convert the answer in no. of

Days	365
Weeks	52
Months	12

20X7	20X8
365/6	365/10
61 days	37 days

Alternatively, inventories days can be calculated directly by:

$$\frac{\text{Cost of sales}}{\text{Inventorie s}} \times 365$$

Reasons for increase in inventory turnover for a given level of inventories

(i)   Increase in demand for goods

(ii)   Goods sold on special offer

(iii)   Increased advertising on special offer

Inventory $10,000

The amount of inventory required and the inventory days, will depend upon the type of company. For example food and vegetable will have low inventory days, whereas a plumbers merchant selling many different fittings may have high inventory days.

1   Too much inventories may result in perishable goods.

2   Money is tied up unnecessarily.

3   Required extra storage space, therefore handling cost will increase, that is insurance cost, storage cost, heating cost and handling cost.

Some companies may deliberately have high inventories if they are planning a major sales drive in the future.

Overdraft $12,000

Overdrafts can be very expensive in interest payments. Overdrafts are repayable on demand. Always reconsider overdraft facility with current assets. (i.e. cancel overdraft if there is another bank account with surplus cash).

Trade payables $5,000

High payables is ok, provided they are not abused (make sure they are paid on time).

Payables days

This ratio helps determine the number of days that is taken by us to pay the suppliers.

Gearing

$$\frac{\text{Debt}}{\text{Debt} + \text{Equity}} \times 100$$

$$\frac{\text{Long - term loan}}{\text{Long - term loan} + \text{Share capital} + \text{Retained earnings} + \text{Other reserves}} \times 100$$

This ratio will determine the level of debt that is used to finance the company, for example the more you borrow, the higher is the gearing. The gearing percentage may also be calculated as Long-term loan/Share capital + Retained earnings + Other reserves i.e. the long-term debt is not included in the denominator.

31   The financial statements of Khan for the year ended 31 December 20X3 are as follows:

Khan

Income statement for the year ended 31 December 20X3

	$	$
Sales		750,000
Less cost of goods sold:		
Opening inventories	190,000	
Purchases	340,000	
Less closing inventories	(170,00)	
	————	(360,000)
		————
Gross profit		390,000
Less expenses		
Selling and delivery costs	160,000	
Administration costs	110,000	
Depreciation	75,000	
	————	(345,000)
		————
Net profit		45,000
		————

Khan

Statement of financial position at 31 December 20X3

Assets	$	$
Non-current assets		
Assets at cost	450,000	
Less acc. depreciation	(180,000)	
	————	270,000
Current assets		
Inventories	150,000	
Receivables and prepayments	80,000	
Bank and cash	20,000	
	————	250,000
		————
		520,000
		————

Capital and liabilities

   Capital at 1 January 20X3   380,000

   Net profit for the year   45,000

   Proprietor's drawings   (25,000)

                                                                         400,000

Current liabilities

   Payables and accruals   120,000

                                                                          520,000

Requirements

Calculate the following accounting ratios from the financial statements presented above:

(i)   Net profit percentage

                   $_____   × 100   =   %

                   $_____

(ii)   Return on capital employed

                   $_____   × 100   =   %

                   $_____

(iii)   Current ratio

                   $_____   =

                   $_____

(iv)   Quick (acid test) ratio

                   $_____   =

                   $_____

Section 2

OBJECTIVE TEST QUESTIONS

THE ACCOUNTING SCENE

1   **Which two of the following are not a profit-making organisation?**

    A   Partnership

    B   Local government

    C   Sole trader

    D   Limited company

    E   Charity

2   **Which one of the following is not a non-profit-making organisation?**

    A   Public limited company

    B   Charity

    C   Clubs

    D   Central government

3   **What is the main aim of financial reporting?**

    A   To record every financial transaction individually

    B   To maintain ledger accounts for every transaction

    C   To prepare a trial balance

    D   To provide financial information to users of such information

4   **Which one of the following gives the best definition of bookkeeping?**

    A   To calculate the amount of dividend to pay to shareholders

    B   To record, categorise and summarise financial transactions

    C   To provide useful information to users

    D   To calculate the taxation due to the government

5 **Which of the following is not an information requirement of equity investors?**

A   Profitability

B   Performance

C   Dividends

D   Ability to repay loans

6 **Which one of the following is not an information requirement of government departments?**

A   Tax on company profits

B   Health and safety

C   Number of employees

D   Payment of dividends

7 **Which of the following is not a qualitative characteristic of financial statements?**

A   Relevance

B   Profitability

C   Comparability

D   Completeness

8 **Which ONE of the following is NOT a purpose of bookkeeping?**

A   maintain ledger accounts for every transaction

B   provide financial information to users of such information

C   prepare a trial balance

D   record every financial transaction individually

9 **The main aim of financial accounting is to**

A   record all transactions in the books of accounts

B   provide management with detailed analyses of costs

C   present the financial results of the organisation by means of recognised statements

D   calculate profit

10 **Financial accounts differ from management accounts in that they**

A   are prepared monthly for internal control purposes

B   contain details of costs incurred in manufacturing

C   are summarised and prepared mainly for external users of accounting information

D   provide information to enable the trial balance to be prepared

11   **Which one of the following does not apply to the preparation of financial statements?**

A   They are prepared annually

B   They provide a summary of the outcome of financial transactions

C   They are prepared mainly for external users of accounting information

D   They are prepared to show the detailed costs of manufacturing and trading

12   **Which of the following statements gives the best definition of the objective of accounting?**

A   To provide useful information to users

B   To record, categorise and summarise financial transactions

C   To calculate the taxation due to the government

D   To calculate the amount of dividend to pay to the shareholders

THE FRAMEWORK OF FINANCIAL STATEMENTS

13   **Which of the following is not part of the income statement?**

A   Sales

B   Gross profit

C   Receivables

D   Rent

14   **Which of the following is not part of the statement of financial position?**

A   Prepayments

B   Short-term loans

C   Interest

D   Payables

15   **Which of the following is not part of the statement of movements on capital?**

A   Capital at the start of the period

B   Net profit earned in the period

C   Non-current assets

D   Capital at the end of the period

16   **Which does not form part of cost of goods?**

A   Closing inventories

B   Sales

C   Opening inventories

D   Purchases

17   Sales $5,000, Purchases $3,000, Closing inventories $2,000, Opening inventories $400. Calculate gross profit/(loss)?

A $3,600 Profit

B $400 Loss

C $10,400 Profit

D $4,400 Loss

18   If the gross profit is $4,300, calculate net profit after the following transactions:

Rent paid $1,000

Interest paid $300

Rent received $200

A $3,000 profit

B $3,200 profit

C $5,600 profit

D $5,800 profit

19   An increase in inventories of $500, a decrease in the bank balance of $800 and an increase in payables of $2,400 results in

A   a decrease in working capital of $2,700

B   an increase in working capital of $2,700

C   a decrease in working capital of $2,100

D   an increase in working capital of $2,100

20   The accounting equation at the start of the month was Assets $14,000 less liabilities $6,250. During the month the following transactions took place: the business purchased a non-current asset for $3,000, paying by cheque, a profit of $3,500 was made and payables of $2,750 were paid by cheque.

Calculate the capital at the end of the month?

A $11,250

B $11,500

C $5,500

D $8,250

21   A sole trader has opening capital of $20,000 and closing capital of $9,000. During the period, the owner introduced capital of $8,000 and withdrew $16,000 for her own use.

Calculate her profit or loss during the period?

A $21,000 loss

B $3,000 profit

C $3,000 loss

D $21,000 profit

22   **The profit of a business may be calculated by using which one of the following formula?**

  A   Opening capital – Drawings + Capital introduced – Closing capital

  B   Opening capital + Drawings – Capital introduced – closing capital

  C   Closing capital + Drawings – Capital introduced – opening capital

  D   Closing capital – Drawings + Capital introduced – Opening capital

23   **Gross profit for 20X1 can be calculated from**

  A   purchases for 20X1 plus inventories at 31 December 20X1 less inventories at 1 January 20X1

  B   purchases for 20X1 less inventories at 31 December 20X1 plus inventories at 1 January 20X1

  C   cost of goods sold during 20X1 plus sales during 20X1

  D   net profit for 20X1 plus expenses for 20X1

24   **The capital of a sole trader would change as a result of**

  A   a payable being paid his account by cheque

  B   raw materials being purchased on credit

  C   non-current assets being purchased on credit

  D   wages being paid in cash

25   **Ricky had a cash balance of $1,000 on 1 June. During June he sold goods on credit for $5,000 and made a profit of $1,000; he bought goods on credit for $2,000; he paid wages of $400. His cash balance on 30 June is $_____**

26   **An increase in receivables of $750, a decrease in the bank overdraft of $400, a decrease in payables of $3,000 and an increase in inventories of $2,000 results in a change of working capital of:**

  increase/decrease_____$_____

27   **The accounting equation can change as a result of certain transactions. Which one of the following transactions would not affect the accounting equation?**

  A   Selling goods for more than their cost

  B   Purchasing a non-current asset on credit

  C   The owner withdrawing cash

  D   Receivables paying their accounts in full, in cash

28   What is meant by the term 'working capital'?

A   Total assets less total liabilities

B   Current assets less current liabilities

C   Capital plus profit less drawings

D   Capital plus profit less drawings plus non-current liabilities

29   Beach's business made sales of $24,000 during the month of January 20X1, indirect expenses amounted to $12,000, and net profit was 10% of sales.

What was the businesses cost of sales for the month?

A $9,600

B $12,000

C $14,400

D $21,600

30   Andy introduces $150,000 into a new business and obtains a loan of $100,000. The net assets of the business are worth:

A $50,000

B $100,000

C $150,000

D $250,000

31   How can we measure the net profit of a trader?

A   Opening capital + drawings — capital introduced — closing capital

B   Closing capital + drawings — capital introduced — opening capital

C   Opening capital — drawings + capital introduced — closing capital

D   Closing capital — drawings + capital introduced — opening capital

32   In a financial year, a business earned $290,000 worth of profit. A further injection of $32,000 was made during the year and inventories worth $8,800 were used for private purposes by the entrepreneur.

Considering the fact that net assets at the beginning of the year were $406,800, the closing net assets should be

A $350,000

B $357,200

C $633,600

D $720,000

33 **If the owner of a business withdraws cash for his personal use, the journal entries will be**

A	Dr Capital	Cr Drawings
B	Dr Cash	Cr Drawings
C	Dr Drawings	Cr Capital
D	Dr Drawings	Cr Cash

34 **Goods withdrawn by a proprietor for his personal use are entered into the books of accounts as:**

A	Dr Drawings	Cr Purchases
B	Dr Purchases	Cr Drawings
C	Dr Capital	Cr Drawings
D	Dr Purchases	Cr Sales

THE ACCOUNTING SYSTEM IN ACTION

35 **A credit balance of $1,834 brought down on B Ltd's account in the books of A Ltd means that**

A   A Ltd owes B Ltd $1,834

B   B Ltd owes A Ltd $1,834

C   A Ltd has paid B Ltd $1,834

D   A Ltd is owed $1,834 by B Ltd

36 **Which one of the following statements is correct?**

A   Assets and liabilities normally have credit balances

B   Liabilities and revenues normally have debit balances

C   Assets and revenues normally have credit balances

D   Assets and expenses normally have debit balances

37 **A credit balance on a ledger account indicates**

A   an asset or an expense

B   a liability or an expense

C   an amount owing to the organisation

D   a liability or revenue

38 On 1 January, a business had a customer, Junior, who owed $1,200. During January, Junior bought goods for $2,100 and returned goods valued at $750. He also paid $960 in cash towards the outstanding balance. The balance of Junior's account on 31 January is

A $1,590 debit

B $1,590 credit

C $810 debit

D $810 credit

39 The correct entries needed to record the return of office equipment that had been bought on credit from Penny, and not yet paid for, are

	Debit	Credit
A	Office equipment	Sales
B	Office equipment	Penny
C	Penny	Office equipment
D	Cash	Office equipment

40 Which one of the following statements regarding the balance on a ledger account is not correct?

A   A credit balance exists where the total of credit entries is more than the total of debit entries

B   A debit balance exists where the total of debit entries is less than the total of credit entries

C   A credit balance exists where the total of debit entries is less than the total of credit entries

D   A debit balance exists where the total of debit entries is more than the total of credit entries

41 Which of the following is the correct entry to record the purchase on credit of inventories intended for resale?

	Debit	Credit
A	Inventories	Receivable
B	Inventories	Payable
C	Purchases	Payable
D	Payable	Purchases

42   X receives goods from Y on credit and X subsequently pays by cheque. X then discovers that the goods are faulty and cancels the cheque before it is cashed by Y. How should X record the cancellation of the cheque in his books?

	Debit	Credit
A	Payables	Returns outwards
B	Payables	Bank
C	Bank	Payables
D	Returns outwards	Payables

43   Jade receives cash from Jose in part-payment of an amount owed to Jade in respect of a sale to Jose. What is the correct double entry?

	Debit	Credit
A	Cash	Sales
B	Cash	Receivables
C	Sales	Cash
D	Payables	Cash

SUMMARISING THE LEDGER ACCOUNTS

44   Where a transaction is credited to the correct purchase ledger account, but debited incorrectly to the repairs and renewals account instead of to plant and machinery account, the error is known as an error of

A   omission

B   commission

C   principle

D   original entry

45   An invoice from a supplier of office equipment has been debited to the stationery account. What is the effect on profit and non-current assets?

Profit

A   Decrease

B   Increase

C   No effect

Non-current assets

A   Decrease

B   Increase

C   No effect

46   The debit side of a trial balance totals $200 more than the credit side. This could be due to

A   a purchase of goods for $200 being omitted from the payables account

B   a sale of goods for $200 being omitted from the receivables account

C   an invoice of $100 for electricity being credited to the electricity account

D   a receipt for $200 from a receivable being omitted from the cash book

47   It is important to produce an opening trial balance prior to preparing the financial statements because

A   it confirms the accuracy of the ledger accounts

B   it provides all the figures necessary to prepare the financial statements

C   it shows that the ledger accounts contain debit and credit entries of an equal value

D   it enables the accountant to calculate any adjustments required

48   An error of original entry would occur if the purchase of goods for resale was

A   debited and credited to the correct accounts using the incorrect amount in both cases

B   credited to the purchases account and debited to the supplier's account

C   debited to a non-current assets account

D   entered correctly in the purchases account, but entered in the supplier's account using the wrong amount

FURTHER ASPECTS OF LEDGER ACCOUNTS

49   Which of the below would represent a cash discount?

A   Discount for payment made in cash

B   Discount for payment made by cheque

C   Discount for payment made before due date

D   Discount for purchases made in bulk

50   What is the double entry for discount allowed?

A   Dr Receivables   Cr Discount allowed

B   Dr Receivables   Cr Discount received

C   Dr Discount allowed   Cr Receivables

D   Dr Discount allowed   Cr Supplier

51   **Where is a discount allowed recognised?**

A   Trading account

B   Income statement

C   Trial balance

D   Statement of financial position

52   **What is the double entry for discount received?**

A   Dr Supplier   Cr Discount received

B   Dr Discount received   Cr Supplier

C   Dr Discount received   Cr Customer

D   Dr Customer   Cr Discount received

53   **Where is a discount received recognised?**

A   Income statement

B   Trading account

C   Statement of financial position

D   Trial balance

54   **Which of the below would represent a trade discount?**

A   Discount for bulk purchases

B   Discount when paying in cash

C   Discount for early settlement of invoice

D   Discount if you trade overseas only

55   **What is the double entry for trade discount?**

A   Dr Sales   Cr Trade discount

B   Dr Trade discount   Cr Sales

C   Dr Purchases   Cr Trade discount

D   No double entry

56   **Where is carriage inwards disclosed?**

A   Income statement

B   Statement of financial position

C   Trading account

D   Trial balance

57   What does carriage inwards effect?

A   Sales

B   Purchases

C   Drawings

D   Capital

58   Carriage outwards is disclosed in

A   Statement of financial position

B   Income statement

C   Trading account

D   Trial balance

59   The cash book of Bright Ltd has a memorandum column recording settlement discounts allowed by suppliers. The column is totalled every week and posted to the nominal ledger.

What is the correct double entry in the nominal ledger?

A   Dr Cash   Cr Discounts received

B   Dr Cash   Cr Discounts allowed

C   Dr Payables   Cr Discounts received

D   Dr Discounts allowed   Cr Receivables

60   A company receives a settlement discount of $1,500 from a supplier. The amount is debited to the discount received account. As a result, gross profit is

A   understated by $1,500

B   understated by $3,000

C   overstated by $3,000

D   unaffected

61   Calculate the sales tax on $100 at rate of 20%

A $20.00

B $16.67

C $120.00

D   Nil

62 How much is the sales tax amount, if gross sales were $100, at a sales tax rate of 20%?

A $20.00

B $16.67

C $120.00

D   Nil

63 X purchased goods costing $500 from Z Ltd (before sales tax at 20%). Z gave X a trade discount of 20%, calculate the net amount after discount.

A $480.00

B $400.00

C $600.00

D $333.33

64 As per Q63, above, calculate sales tax at 20% on purchases after trade discount.

A $100.00

B $80.00

C $20.00

D $94.00

65 As per Q63, above, what would be the final double entry after calculation of trade discount and sales tax at 20%?

			£	£
A	Dr	Purchases	400	
	Dr	Sales tax	80	
	Cr	Supplier		480
B	Dr	Supplier	480	
	Cr	Sales tax		80
	Cr	Purchases		400
C	Dr	Purchase	600	
	Dr	Sales tax	100	
	Cr	Supplier		700
D	Dr	Purchases	480	
	Dr	Sales tax	100	
	Cr	Supplier		580

66 Which of the following transactions would result in an increase in capital employed?

A   Selling inventories at profit

B   Writing off a bad debt

C   Paying a payable in cash

D   Increasing the bank overdraft to purchase a non-current asset

67 Rent paid on 1 October 20X2 for the year to September 20X3 was $600 and rent paid on 1 October 20X3 for the year to 30 September 20X4 was $800. Rent payable, as shown in the income statement for the year ended 31 December 20X3, would be

A $600

B $800

C $650

D $750

68 Norman commenced business on 1 May 20X0 and is charged rent at the rate of $18,000 per annum.

During the period to 31 December 20X0 he actually paid $13,800.

What should his charge in the income statement be in respect of rent?

69 A decrease in the allowance for receivables would result in

A   an increase in liabilities

B   a decrease in working capital

C   a decrease in net profit

D   an increase in net profit

70 The sales account is

A   credited with the total of sales made, including sales tax

B   credited with the total of sales made, excluding sales tax

C   debited with the total of sales made, including sales tax

D   debited with the total of sales made, excluding sales tax

71 An employee is paid at the rate of $20 per hour. Earnings of more than $300 a week are taxed at 20%. Employees' social security tax is 8%, and employer's social security tax is 12%. During week 42, the employee works for 45 hours.

The amounts to be charged to the income statement and paid to the employee are:

Income statement	Paid to employee
$	$

72 Triangle purchases inventories with a list price of $120,000. The supplier grants a trade discount of 5% on list price, and Triangle also takes advantage of a cash discount amounting to 2% of list price.

In Triangle's statement of financial position the amount of the inventories should be

A $108,000

B $114,000

C $102,600

D $120,000

ACCOUNTING FOR NON-CURRENT ASSETS

73 Your firm bought a machine for $15,000 on 1 January 2001, which had an expected useful life of four years and an expected residual value of $3,000; the asset was to be depreciated on the straight-line basis. On 31 December 2003, the machine was sold for $4,800. What is the amount to be entered in the 2003 income statement account for profit or loss on disposal?

74 The most appropriate definition of depreciation is

A a means of determining the decrease in market value of an asset over time

B a means of allocating the cost of an asset over a number of accounting periods

C a means of setting funds aside for the replacement of the asset

D a means of estimating the current value of the asset

75 A business buys a machine for $120,000 on 1 January 20X3 and another one on 1 July 20X3 for $144,000. Depreciation is charged at 10% per annum on cost, and calculated on a monthly basis. What is the total depreciation charge for the two machines for the year ended 31 December 20X3?

A $13,200

B $19,200

C $21,600

D $26,400

76 The purpose of charging depreciation on non-current assets is

A to put money aside to replace the assets when required

B to show the assets in the statement of financial position at their fair value

C to ensure that the profit is not understated

D to spread the net cost of the assets over their estimated useful life

77 The phrase 'carrying amount' when applied to tangible non-current assets means that

A the assets are shown in the statement of financial position at their original cost

B the assets are valued at their likely selling price

C the assets have been depreciated using the reducing balance method

D the assets are shown in the statement of financial position at their cost less accumulated depreciation

78   Ellison & Partners bought machinery for $300,000 on 1 January 20X5, and have depreciated it at 10% per annum by the reducing instalment method.

What is the depreciation charge for the year ended 31 December 20X7?

A $21,870

B $24,300

C $27,000

D $30,000

79   Gene's business bought a machine for $72,000 on 1 January 20X0 and another one for $96,000 on 1 July 20X0. Depreciation is charged at 10% per annum straight line and calculated on a monthly basis.

What is the total depreciation charge for the two machines for the year ended 31 December 20X0?

A $6,000

B $8,400

C $12,000

D $16,800

80   Which of the following statements regarding goodwill is not correct?

A   Goodwill is classified as an intangible non-current asset

B   Goodwill is the excess of the value of a business as a whole over the fair value of its separable net assets

C   Purchased goodwill may be shown on the statement of financial position and is subject to regular impairment reviews

D   Non-purchased goodwill is a liability

81   We Ltd bought a new printing machine from abroad. The cost of the machine was $40,000. The installation costs were $2,500 and the employees received specific training on how to use this particular machine at a cost of $1,000. Before using the machine to print customers' orders, a test was undertaken and the paper and ink cost was $500. What should be the cost of the machine in the company's statement of financial position?

82   The reducing-balance method of depreciating non-current asset is more appropriate than the straight-line method when

A   the expected life of the asset is short

B   the asset is expected to decrease in value by a non-current percentage of cost each year

C   the expected life of the asset cannot be estimated accurately

D   it better reflects the pattern of the consumption of the economic benefits derived from the asset

ORGANISING THE BOOKKEEPING SYSTEM

83 **A book of prime entry is one in which:**

   A   The rules of double-entry bookkeeping do not apply

   B   Ledger accounts are maintained

   C   Transactions are entered prior to being recorded in the ledger accounts

   D   Subsidiary accounts are kept

84 **Which one of the following is a book of prime entry and part of the double-entry system?**

   A   The journal

   B   The petty cash book

   C   The sales day book

   D   The purchase ledger

85 **The petty-cash imprest is restored to $300 at the end of each week. The following amounts are paid out of petty cash during week 23:**

   Stationery $42.30 including sales tax at 20%
   Travelling costs $76.50
   Office refreshments $38.70
   Sundry payables $72.00 plus sales tax at 20%

   What is the amount required to restore the imprest to $300?

86 **Inventory is measured using FIFO. Opening inventory was 10 units at $4 each. Purchases were 30 units at $6 each, then issues of 12 units were made, followed by issues of 8 units. Closing inventory is valued at $.............**

87 **In times of rising prices, the FIFO method of inventories valuation, when compared with the average cost method of inventories valuation, will usually produce**

   A   a higher profit and lower closing inventories value

   B   a higher profit and a higher closing inventories value

   C   a lower profit and a lower closing inventories value

   D   a lower profit and a higher closing inventories value

88 **Inventory movements for product X during the last quarter were as follows:**

   Opening inventories   6 items at $30.00 each

   January   Purchases   10 items at $39.60 each
   February   Sales   10 items at $60 each
   March   Purchases   20 items at $49 each
                Sales   5 items at $60 each

   Gross profit for the quarter, using the weighted average cost method, would be $..........

89 A firm uses the LIFO cost formula. Information regarding inventories movements during a particular month are as follows:

1	Opening balance	300 units valued at $3,000
10	Purchases	700 units for $8,400
14	Sales	400 units for $8,000
21	Purchases	600 units for $9,000
23	Sales	800 units for $17,600

The cost of inventories at the end of the month would be:

$ ....

90 S & Co. sells three products – Small, Medium and Large. The following information was available at the year-end:

	Small	Medium	Large
	$ per unit	$ per unit	$ PER UNIT
Original cost	10	15	20
Estimated selling price	14	18	19
Selling and distribution costs	1	4	3
	Units	Units	Units
Units in inventories	300	400	600

The value of inventories at the year end should be:

$ ....

91 An organisation's cash book has an opening balance in the bank column of $900 credit. 'The following transactions then took place:

- cash sales $2,300 including sales tax of $300;
- receipts from customers of $7,200;
- payments to payables of $5,000 less 5% cash discount;
- dishonoured cheques from customers amounting to $400.

The closing balance in the bank column of the cash book should be:

$ ....

CONTROLLING THE BOOKKEEPING SYSTEM

92 What effect on a positive cash balance does an adjustment for unpresented paid cheques have on a bank reconciliation?

A   Increase in the cash book balance

B   Decrease in the cash book balance

C   Increase in the balance shown by the bank statement

D   Decrease in the balance shown by the bank statement

93 The cash book shows a bank balance of $6,800 overdrawn at 31 July 20X9. It is subsequently discovered that a standing order for $300 has been entered twice, and that a dishonoured cheque for $750 has been debited in the cash book instead of credited. The correct bank balance should be:

$ ....

94 Andrew has just completed the following reconciliation of the bank statement to his cash book.

Bank reconciliation statement as at 31 December 20X5

	$
Balance as per bank statement	9,564
Add: Unpresented cheques	772
	10,336
Less: Uncleared lodgements	(218)
Balance as per cash book	10,118

What figure for cash should be included in the trial balance at 31 December 20X5?

A $9,564 Dr

B $9,564 Cr

C $10,118 Dr

D $10,118 Cr

95 A supplier sends you a statement showing a balance outstanding of $6,850. Your own records show a balance outstanding of $7,500. The reason for this difference could be that:

A   the supplier sent an invoice for $650 that you have not yet received

B   the supplier has allowed you $650 cash discount that you had omitted to enter in your ledgers

C   you have paid the supplier $650 that he has not yet accounted for

D   you have returned goods worth $650 that the supplier has not yet accounted for

96 After calculating your company's profit for 20X9, you discover that:

• The purchase of goods for $3,400 has been included in a non-current asset ledger account.

• Interest received of $400 has been credited to sales.

The correction of these errors will be:

	Gross profit $	Net profit $
Increase/decrease		

97 Ali's business had receivables of $1,950 at 1 January 20X3 and $1,200 at 31 December 20X3. $96,750 was received from customers on credit during the year.

Assuming that there were no bad debts and no discounts allowed, what were credit sales for the year?

A $96,000

B $96,750

C $97,200

D $97,950

98 Which of the following is not the purpose of a sales ledger control account?

A   A sales ledger control account ensures that there are no errors in the personal ledger

B   Control accounts deter fraud

C   A sales ledger control account provides a check on the arithmetic accuracy of the personal ledger

D   A sales ledger control account helps to locate errors in the trial balance

99 Allot's business had receivables of $300 at 1 January 20X4 and $270 at 31 December 20X4. Credit sales amounted to $2,370 and cash received from receivables was $2,310; a bad debt of $30 was written off.

How much discount was allowed to customers during the year?

A $60

B $120

C $210

D $270

100 From the following information, calculate the value of purchases:

	$
Opening payables	71,300
Cash paid to suppliers	271,150
Discounts received	6,600
Goods returned	13,750
Closing payables	68,900

101 A suspense account shows a credit balance of $260.

This could be due to

A   omitting a sale of $260 from the sales ledger

B   recording a purchase of $260 twice in the purchases account

C   failing to write off a bad debt of $260

D   recording an electricity bill paid of $130 by debiting the bank account and crediting the electricity account

102 You are given the following information:

	$
Receivables at 1 January 2003	30,000
Receivables at 31 December 2003	27,000
Total receipts during 2003 (including cash sales of $15,000)	255,000

Sales on credit during 2003 amount to $..................

103 A contra entry for $1,912 had been fully recorded in the books, with the payables' ledger entry being in the account of Harry and the receivables' ledger entry being in the account of Carry. This contra, which should never have been made, is to be cancelled. What will the impact of the required correction be?

	Purchase ledger control account	List of supplier balances
A	No effect	Increase total by $1,912
B	Credit $1,912	Increase total by $1,912
C	Debit $1,912	Decrease total by $1,912
D	No effect	Decrease total by $1,912

104 A total, $19,400, from the payments side of the cash book had been posted to the credit side of the payables' ledger control account. What journal entry is required to correct this error?

	Debit	Credit
A	Payables' ledger control $19,400	Suspense account $19,400
B	Suspense account $19,400	Payables' ledger control $19,400
C	Payables' ledger control $38,800	Suspense account $38,800
D	Suspense account $38,800	Payables' ledger control $38,800

105 A payment of $240 from petty cash for stationery had been entered in the books twice. What adjustment is required to correct this?

	Debit	Credit
A	Stationery account $240	Suspense account $240
B	Stationery account $240	Petty cash $240
C	Suspense account $240	Stationery account $240
D	Petty cash $240	Stationery account $240

106 Which of the following errors would cause an entry to be made in a suspense account?

A Rent charges debited to the local business tax account

B Cash paid to a payable debited to the wrong payable's account

C Cash received from a receivable debited to the wrong receivable's account

D Purchase of goods by the business for the proprietor's private consumption debited to purchases

107 A sales day book total of $2,160 had been posted to the sales account as $1,260, but had been entered correctly in the receivables' ledger control account. What adjustment is required to correct this?

	Debit	Credit
A	Suspense account $900	Sales account $900
B	Sales account $900	Suspense account $900
C	Suspense account $1,800	Sales account $1,800
D	Sales account $1,800	Suspense account $1,800

108 The purchase of office equipment for $750 had been charged to the purchases account. What adjustment is required to correct this?

	Debit	Credit
A	Office equipment account $750	Suspense account $750
B	Purchase account $750	Office equipment account $750
C	Suspense account $750	Purchase account $750
D	Office equipment account $750	Purchase account $750

109 Faulty goods returned by a customer with a sales value of $37 had been correctly treated in his personal account and in the receivables' ledger control account, but had been credited to the sales returns account as $73. What adjustment is required to correct this?

	Debit	Credit
A	Sales returns account $36	Suspense account $36
B	Suspense account $36	Sales returns account $36
C	Sales returns account $110	Suspense account $110
D	Suspense account $110	Sales returns account $110

110 After the draft financial statements of Cats Ltd have been prepared, some inventories are found in an old shed which was not included in the physical inventory count. It appears that they originally cost $1,000, but it was thought that they will fetch only $100.

What is the effect on the company's gross profit?

A   Increase $100

B   Decrease $900

C   Increase $1,000

D   Decrease $1,000

111 Your firm's cash book shows a credit balance of $2,480 at 30 April 20X9. Upon comparison with the bank statement, you determine that there are unpresented cheques totalling $450, and a receipt of $140 that has not yet been passed through the bank account. The bank statement shows bank charges of $75 that have not been entered. The balance on the bank statement is $ _____

112 **A company's cash book at 31 December 20X4 shows a debit balance of $2,125. When the bank statement as at that date is received it is found that cheques drawn by the company totalling $274 had not been presented. In addition, the statement recorded bank charges of $58 which had not been entered in the cash book.**

What was the balance on the bank statement as at 31 December 20X4?

A $1,909 overdrawn balance

B $1,909 favourable balance

C $2,341 favourable balance

D $2,457 favourable balance

THE REGULATORY FRAMEWORK OF ACCOUNTING

113 **If, at the end of the financial year, a company makes a charge against the profit for stationery consumed but not yet invoiced, this adjustment is in accordance with the convention:**

A   materiality

B   accruals

C   consistency

D   objectivity

114 **The historical cost convention**

A   fails to take account of changing price levels over time

B   records only past transactions

C   values all assets at their cost to the business, without any adjustment for depreciation

D   has been replaced in accounting records by a system of current cost accounting

115 **In times of rising prices, the historical cost convention has the effect of**

A   valuing all assets at their cost to the business

B   recording goods sold at their cost price, even if they are worth less than that cost

C   understating profits and overstating statement of financial position asset values

D   overstating profits and understating statement of financial position asset values

116 **Sales revenue should be recognised only when goods and services have been supplied.**

The accounting convention that governs the above is the

A   accruals convention

B   materiality convention

C   realisation convention

D   dual aspect convention

117   **The capital maintenance implies that**

  A   the capital of a business should be kept intact by not paying our dividends

  B   a business should invest its profits in the purchase of capital assets

  C   non-current assets should be properly maintained

  D   profit is earned only if the value of an organisation's net assets or its operating capability has increased during the accounting period

118   **The accounting convention that dictates that non-current assets should be valued at cost less accumulated depreciation, rather than their enforced saleable value, is the**

  A   net realisable value convention

  B   prudence convention

  C   realisation convention

  D   going concern convention

119   **Goodwill is most appropriately classed as**

  A   a current asset

  B   an intangible asset

  C   a fictitious liability

  D   a semi-non-current asset

120   **A major aim of the internal auditors is to**

  A   reduce the costs of the external auditors by carrying out some of their duties

  B   report to management on internal controls

  C   prepare the financial accounts

  D   report to shareholders on the accuracy of the financial statements

121   **Which one of the following is not a necessary part of the stewardship function?**

  A   To maximise profits

  B   To safeguard assets

  C   To ensure adequate controls exist to prevent or detect fraud

  D   To prepare the financial accounts

122   **Who issues International Financial Reporting Standards?**

  A   The International Auditing and Assurance Standards Board

  B   The Stock Exchange

  C   The International Accounting Standards Board

  D   The Government

123 **Which of the following is not an accounting convention?**

A   Prudence

B   Consistency

C   Depreciation

D   Accruals

124 **When preparing financial statements in periods of inflation, directors**

A   must reduce asset values

B   must increase asset values

C   must reduce dividends

D   need make no adjustments

125 **Which of the following statements is correct?**

A   External auditors report to the directors

B   External auditors are appointed by the directors

C   External auditors are required to give a report to shareholders

D   External auditors correct errors in financial statements

126 **What is an audit trail in a computerised accounting system?**

A   A list of all the transactions in a period

B   A list of all the transactions in a ledger account in a period

C   A list of all the items checked by the auditor

D   A list of all the nominal ledger codes

127 **Capital maintenance is important for**

A   the sources of finance

B   the measurement of profit

C   the relationship of debt to equity

D   the purchase of non-current assets

128 **Internal controls includes 'detect' control and 'prevent' control. Which of the following is a detect control?**

A   Signing overtime claim forms

B   Matching purchase invoices with goods received notes

C   Preparing bank reconciliations

D   Matching sales invoices with delivery notes

129 **The fundamental objective of an external audit of a limited company is to**

A   give advice to shareholders

B   detect fraud and errors

C   measure the performance and financial position of a company

D   provide an opinion on the financial statements

130 **Which one of the following statements most closely expresses the meaning of 'true and fair'?**

A   There is only one true and fair view of a company's financial statements

B   True and fair is determined by compliance with accounting conventions

C   True and fair is determined by compliance with company law

D   True and fair is largely determined by compliance with international accounting standards

131 **A company includes in inventories goods received before the year end, but for which invoices are not received until after the year end. This is in accordance with**

A   the historical cost convention

B   the accruals convention

C   the consistency convention

D   the materiality convention

132 **Which of the following is not correct?**

A   Depreciation reduces the net profit of an organisation

B   Providing depreciation generates cash

C   If depreciation is not charged, capital will not be maintained

D   By not charging depreciation, it might appear that profits have risen in line with inflation

133 **Your company auditor insists that it is necessary to record items of plant separately and to depreciate them over several years, but that items of office equipment, such as hand-held stapling machines, can be grouped together and written off against profits immediately.**

The main reason for this difference in treatment between the two items is because

A   treatments of the two items must be consistent with treatment in previous years

B   items of plant last for several years, whereas hand-held stapling machines last only for months

C   hand-held stapling machines are not regarded as material items

D   items of plant are revalued from time to time, whereas hand-held stapling machines are recorded at historical cost

INCOMPLETE RECORDS AND INCOME AND EXPENDITURE STATEMENTS

134 **In a not-for-profit organisation, the accumulated fund is**

 A non-current liabilities plus current liabilities plus current assets

 B non-current assets less current liabilities less non-current liabilities

 C the balance on the general reserve account

 D non-current assets plus net current assets less non-current liabilities

135 **An income and expenditure statement is**

 A a summary of the cash and bank transactions for a period

 B another name for a receipts and payments account

 C similar to an income statement in reflecting revenue earned and expenses

 D incurred during a period

136 A club received subscriptions during 2005 totalling $25,000. Of these, $1,600 related to 2004 and $800 related to 2006. There were subscriptions in arrears at the end of 2005 of $500. What total for subscriptions should be included in the income and expenditure statement for 2005?

137 **Life membership fees payable to a club are usually dealt with by**

 A crediting the total received to a life membership fees account and transferring a proportion each year to the income and expenditure statement

 B crediting the total received to the income and expenditure statement in the year in which these fees are received

 C debiting the total received to a life membership fees account and transferring a proportion each year to the income and expenditure statement

 D debiting the total received to the income and expenditure statement in the year in which these fees are received

138 **A receipts and payments account is similar to**

 A an income and expenditure statement

 B an income statement

 C a trading account

 D a cash book summary

139 **The subscriptions receivable account of a club commenced the year with subscriptions in arrears of $250 and subscriptions in advance of $375. During the year, $62,250 was received in subscriptions, including all of the arrears and $600 for next year's subscriptions. The amount to be taken to the income and expenditure statement for the year is $....................**

140 A club takes no credit for subscriptions due until they are received. On 1 January 20X5 arrears of subscriptions amounted to $24 and subscriptions paid in advance were $14. On 31 December 20X5 the amounts were $42 and $58, respectively. Subscription receipts during the year were $1,024.

In the income and expenditure statement for 20X5 the income from subscriptions would be shown as:

A $956

B $980

C $998

D $1,050

THE MANUFACTURING ACCOUNT

141 The following information relates to a company at its year end:

	$
Inventories at beginning of year	
Raw materials	20,000
Work-in-progress	4,000
Finished goods	68,000
Inventories at end of year	
Raw materials	22,000
Work-in-progress	8,000
Finished goods	60,000
Purchase of raw materials	100,000
Direct wages	80,000
Royalties on goods sold	6,000
Production overheads	120,000
Distribution costs	110,000
Administration expenses	140,000
Sales	600,000

The cost of goods manufactured during the year is $.....................

142 If work-in-progress decreases during the period, then:

A   prime cost will decrease

B   prime cost will increase

C   the factory cost of goods completed will decrease

D   the factory cost of goods completed will increase

143 The cost of royalties paid on goods manufactured is included in:

A   factory overheads

B   selling and distribution expenses

C   prime cost

D   trading account

144 The prime cost of goods manufactured is the total of:

A   all factory costs before adjusting for work-in-progress

B   all factory costs of goods completed

C   all materials and labour

D   direct factory costs

145 Which one of the following costs would not be shown as a factory overhead in a manufacturing account?

A   The cost of insurance on a factory

B   The cost of an extension to a factory

C   The cost of depreciation on a factory

D   The cost of rent on a factory

THE FINANCIAL STATEMENTS OF LIMITED COMPANIES AND STATEMENT OF CASH FLOWS

146 Revenue reserves are

A   accumulated and undistributed profits of a company

B   amounts that cannot be distributed as dividends

C   amounts set aside out of profits to replace revenue items

D   amounts set aside out of profits for a specific purpose

147 The correct ledger entries needed to record the issue of $400,000 $1 shares at a premium of 60c, and paid for by cheque, in full, would be

	Debit	Credit
	$	$
Bank		
Share premium		
Share capital		

148   Which one of the following would you expect to find in the statement of changes in equity of a limited company, for the current year?

    A   Ordinary dividend proposed during the previous year, but paid in the current year

    B   Ordinary dividend proposed during the current year, but paid in the following year

    C   Directors' fees

    D   Auditors' fees

149   A business has made a profit of $4,000 but its bank balance has fallen by $2,500. This could be due to

    A   depreciation of $1,500 and an increase in inventories of $5,000

    B   depreciation of $3,000 and the repayment of a loan of $3,500

    C   depreciation of $6,000 and the purchase of new non-current assets for $12,500

    D   the disposal of a non-current asset for $6,500 less than its carrying amount

150   The record of how the profit or loss of a company has been allocated to distributions and reserves is found in the

    A   capital account

    B   statement of comprehensive income

    C   reserves account

    D   statement of changes in equity

151   Revenue reserve would decrease if a company

    A   sets aside profits to purchase future non-current assets

    B   transfers amounts into 'general reserves'

    C   issues shares at a premium

    D   pays dividend

152   Which one of the following does not form part of the equity capital of a limited company?

    A   Debentures

    B   Share premium

    C   Revaluation reserve

    D   Ordinary share capital

153   If a company pays 10% dividend, what is this a percentage of?

    A   profit before tax

    B   profit after tax

    C   authorised share capital

    D   issued share capital

154 **In a statement of comprehensive income, the difference between 'profit for the period' and 'total comprehensive income for the period' is:**

A   Interest paid

B   Income tax

C   Gains on revaluation of property

D   Dividends

155 **Which two of the following items would you not expect to find in a statement of changes in equity?**

A   Dividends

B   Transfer between reserves

C   Gains on revaluation of property

D   Issue of shares

E   Income tax

F   Total comprehensive income

156 **What is a reserve?**

A   an asset

B   a liability

C   a charge against profit

D   equity

157 **Bill Limited shows the following items as 'reserves' in its financial statements. Which one of them is wrongly classified?**

A   retained earnings

B   allowance for receivables

C   general reserve

D   share premium account

158 **The estimated income tax charges of Cherry Limited for the years ended 31 December 20X6 and 31 December 20X7 were $2,400 and $2,700, respectively. However, the final settlements were $2,200 and $2,800, respectively.**

What was the total income tax charge shown in the income statement of Cherry Limited for the year ended 31 December 20X7?

A $2,500

B $2,600

C $2,700

D $2,800

159 **With regards to a statement of cash flows, which of the following statements is correct?**

A   Dividends declared are an outflow of cash under the heading 'financing activities'

B   Dividends proposed are an outflow of cash under the heading 'financing activities'

C   Dividends paid are an outflow of cash under the heading 'financing activities'

D   Dividends paid are an outflow of cash under the heading 'investing activities'

160 **When a shareholder in a limited company sells his shares to another private investor for less than what he paid for them, the share capital of the company will**

A   fall by the nominal value of the shares

B   increase by the nominal value of the shares

C   increase by the amount received for the shares

D   remain unchanged

161 **Which one of the following is not a revenue reserve?**

A   Retained earnings

B   General reserve

C   Specific reserve to replace non-current assets

D   Share premium

162 **Which one of the following statements with regard to dividends is true?**

A   Proposed dividends do not appear in financial statements

B   Declared dividends do not appear in financial statements

C   Directors have to pay a dividend if there is a profit

D   Companies always pay dividends in two instalments – interim and final

163 **A statement of cash flows can best be described as**

A   a statement showing the effects of profit on cash resources

B   a statement of cash inflows and outflows from operating activities

C   a statement showing the movement in working capital

D   a statement showing the inflows and outflows of cash

164 **Revenue reserves would increase if a company**

A   issued shares at a premium

B   makes a transfer from retained profit earnings to general reserves

C   Increases retained earnings

D   increases its current bank balances

165 **Total comprehensive income is:**

A   Profit before tax

B   Profit plus other comprehensive income

C   Profit before interest paid

D   Profit for the period

THE INTERPRETATION OF FINANCIAL STATEMENTS

166 **Given selling price of $700 and gross profit mark-up of 40%, the cost price would be $.............**

167 **Sales are $220,000. Purchases are $160,000. Opening inventories is $24,000. Closing inventory is $20,000. The rate of inventory turnover is**

.... times (to 1 decimal place)

168 **The formula for calculating the rate of inventory turnover is**

A   average inventories at cost divided by cost of goods sold

B   sales divided by average inventories at cost

C   sales divided by average inventories at selling price

D   cost of goods sold divided by average inventories at cost

169 **A company's gearing ratio would rise if**

A   a decrease in long-term loans is less than a decrease in shareholder's funds

B   a decrease in long-term loans is more than a decrease in shareholder's funds

C   interest rates rose

D   interest rates fell

170 **A company has the following details extracted from its statement of financial position:**

	$000
Inventory	3,800
Receivables	2,000
Bank overdraft	200
Payables	2,000

What is:

(a)   the current ratio?

(b)   the quick (acid test) ratio?

Express your answer to 1 decimal place.

171 **Revenue reserves would decrease if a company**

A   sets aside profits to pay future dividends

B   transfers amounts into 'general reserves'

C   issues shares at a premium

D   pays dividends

172 **The accountant of Aina Limited gives you the following information for the year ended 31 December 20X7:**

Inventories at 1 January	$9,075
Inventories at 31 December	$4,500
Purchases	$36,325
Gross profit margin	30%

What was the company's gross profit for the year?

A $12,270

B $13,608

C $15,567

D $17,529

Data for questions 173–178

The trading account of Calypso Ltd for the year ended 30 June 20X5 is set out below:

	$	$
Sales		430,000
Opening inventories	50,000	
Purchases	312,500	
	362,500	
Closing inventories	(38,000)	
Cost of sales		(324,500)
Gross profit		105,500

The following amounts have been extracted from the company's statement of financial position at 30 June 20X5.

	$
Trade receivables	60,000
Prepayments	4,000
Cash in hand	6,000
Bank overdraft	8,000
Trade Payables	40,000
Accruals	3,000
Declared dividends	5,000

In the questions that follow assume a year to be 365 days and ignore sales tax.

173 **Calculate the inventories days, using average inventories.**

A   33 days

B   17 days

C   49 days

D   51 days

174 **Calculate receivables days.**

A   51 days

B   54 days

C   67 days

D   72 days

175 **Calculate payables days.**

A   45 days

B   47 days

C   50 days

D   78 days

176 **Calculate the current ratio.**

A   1.25:1

B   1.93:1

C   2.04:1

D   2.12:1

177 **Calculate the quick ratio (or acid test ratio).**

A   1.25:1

B   1.28:1

C   1.37:1

D   1.50:1

178 **Calculate the length of the cash cycle in days.**

A   2 days

B   4 days

C   53 days

D   100 days

Data for questions 179–182

The following information has been derived from the financial statements of Montgomery plc for the year ended 31 December 20X5.

On 31 December 20X5

Current ratio	1.4:1
Quick ratio	0.9:1
Current assets minus current liabilities	$32,000
Receivables collection period	6 weeks

For the year ended 31 December 20X5

Operating profit for the year as a percentage of ordinary share capital in issue	40%
Annual rate of inventories turnover	8.775 times
Gross profit as a percentage of sales	25%

On 31 December 20X5 there were no current assets other than inventories, receivables and bank balances and no liabilities other than current liabilities. Assume a 52-week year.

179 Calculate the amount of Montgomery plc's current liabilities on 31 December 20X5.

    A $22,857

    B $28,800

    C $44,800

    D $80,000

180 Calculate the amount of Montgomery plc's inventories at 31 December 20X5.

    A $16,000

    B $32,000

    C $40,000

    D $56,000

181 Calculate Montgomery plc's revenue for 20X5.

    A $351,000

    B $437,500

    C $438,500

    D $468,000

182 Calculate Montgomery plc's bank balance at 31 December 20X5.

    A $18,000

    B $48,000

    C $54,000

    D $72,000

Section 3

ANSWERS TO PRACTICE QUESTIONS

THE FRAMEWORK OF FINANCIAL STATEMENTS

1

	Assets	Liabilities	Capital
	$	$	$
(i)	50,000	7,200	**42,800**
(ii)	112,000	19,600	**92,400**
(iii)	67,200	**17,200**	50,000
(iv)	96,400	**30,600**	65,800
(v)	**102,000**	25,200	76,800
(vi)	**209,600**	50,600	159,000

2

(i)	Asset	(vii)	Asset
(ii)	*Liability*	(viii)	*Liability*
(iii)	Asset	(ix)	*Liability*
(iv)	Asset	(x)	Asset
(v)	*Liability*	(xi)	*Liability*
(vi)	Asset	(xii)	Asset

3

Assets		*Liabilities*	
Loan from A Lamb	Wrong	Receivables	Wrong
Motor Vehicles		Money owing to bank	
Premises		Inventories	Wrong
Goodwill		Loan from Riffle	
Machinery		Money owing to A Little	
Cash in hand		Fixtures	Wrong
Capital	Wrong	Payables	
Cash at bank		Buildings	Wrong

4   Total Assets = Liabilities + Capital

Fixtures	12,000	Payables	8,400
Motor vehicle	30,000	Brother's loan	18,000
Inventories	21,000	Capital	?????
Bank	16,800		
Cash in hand	600		
	_____		_____
	80,400		80,400
	_____		_____

Hence Capital = Assets − Liabilities = 80,400 − 26,400 = 54,000

THE ACCOUNTING SYSTEM IN ACTION

5   (i)   Debit

(ii)   Credit

(iii)   Debit

(iv)   Credit

(v)   Credit

(vi)   Debit

(vii)   Debit

(viii)   Debit

(ix)   Credit

(x)   Credit

6

		Account to be debited	Account to be credited
(i)	Goods bought on credit from S Davis	Purchase	Davis
(ii)	Goods returned to us by H Higgins	Return inward	H Higgins
(iii)	Machinery returned to A Snooker Ltd	A Snooker	Return outward
(iv)	Goods bought for cash	Purchases	Cash
(v)	Motor van bought on credit from I Landle	Purchases	I Landle
(vi)	Goods returned by us to B Boro	B Boro	Return outward
(vii)	J McEnroe paid up his account by cheque	Bank	J McEnroe
(viii)	Goods bought by cheque	Purchases	Bank
(ix)	We paid payable, S Graf by cheque	S Graf	Bank
(x)	Goods sold on credit to J Muller	J Muller	Sales

7   **Comprehensive example (Sport stars)**

Purchases

		$		$
Sep 1	D Underwood	68		
Sep 2	M Hughes	154		
Sep 12	Cash	100		
Sep 30	M Hughes	128		

Sales

	$			$
		Sep 5	A Border	60
		Sep 6	A Steward	50
		Sep 21	Cash	150

Return inwards

		$		$
Sep 19	A Steward	16		

Return outwards

	$			$
		Sep 10	D Underwood	14

D Underwood

		$			$
Sep 10	Return outward	14	Sep 1	Purchases	68
Sep 22	Cash	54			

A Border

		$			$
Sep 5	Sales	60	Sep 30	Cash	60

A Steward

		$			$
Sep 6	Sales	50	Sep 19	Return inwards	16

Cash

		$			$
Sep 21	Sales	150	Sep 12	Purchases	100
Sep 30	A Border	60	Sep 22	D Underwood	54

M Hughes

	$			$
		Sep 2	Purchases	154
		Sep 30	Purchases	128

SUMMARISING THE LEDGER ACCOUNTS

8   Trial balance is a list of balances in a double entry bookkeeping system. If the records have been correctly maintained, the sum of the debit balances will equal the sum of the credit balances although certain errors, such as errors of omission of transactions or erroneous entries, will not be disclosed by the trial balance.

9   Trial balance is thus a list of balances on the ledger accounts. If the totals of the debit and credit balances on the trial balance are not equal, then an error or errors have been made either:

(a)   in the posting of the transactions to the ledger accounts or

(b)   in balancing of the accounts or

(c)   in the transferring of the balances from the ledger account to the trial balance.

10   Error of omission – where the transaction has been completely omitted from the ledger accounts.

Error of commission – where one side of the transaction has been entered in wrong account (will not affect profit or statement of financial position).

Error of original entry – where the wrong amount has been used for both debit and credit side.

Error of principle – as for errors of commission, but the correct and incorrect amounts are of different types, for example entered in purchase account instead of non-current asset account.

ACCOUNTING FOR NON-CURRENT ASSETS

11   Straight-line, Reducing balance, Usage, Revaluation.

12   **A**

C and D are incorrect as asset is not a inventory item and hence cannot be purchased unless it is purchased for resale.

13

	Dr	Cr
	$	$
Cost of NCA		X
Cum Depn NCA	X	
Bank		X
Disposal account	X	

PREPARATION OF FINANCIAL STATEMENTS WITH ADJUSTMENTS

14   NICO

Income statement for the year ended 31 July 20X9

	$	$
Sales		150,000
Opening inventories	10,000	
Purchases	40,000	
	50,000	
Closing inventories	(12,000)	
Cost of goods sold		(38,000)
Gross profit		112,000
Selling and distribution (£50,000 + £4,000)	54,000	
Administration (£15,000 – £6,000)	9,000	
Bad debts (£15,000 × 5% = £750 – £2,000)	(1,250)	
Depreciation	15,000	
Interest	1,600	
		(78,350)
Net profit		33,650

NICO

Statement of financial position at 31 July 20X9

	Cost	Acc. Depn.	Carrying amount $
ASSETS			
Non-current assets			
Plant and machinery	155,000	(65,000)	90,000
Current Assets			
Inventories		12,000	
Receivables	15,000		
Less allowance	(750)	14,250	
Prepayment		6,000	
Bank		3,400	
			35,650
			125,650

CAPITAL AND LIABILITIES

Capital at 1 August 20X8		100,000
Profit for the year	33,650	
Less drawings	(35,000)	(1,350)
		98,650
Non-current liability		
Bank loan – repayable 2015		20,000
Current liabilities		
Trade payables	3,000	
Accruals	4,000	7,000
		125,650

15   A1 Alarms

Income statement year ended 31 August 20X3

		$
Sales		382,000
Opening inventories	24,000	
Purchases	240,000	
	264,000	
Closing inventories	(20,000)	
Cost of goods sold		(244,000)
Gross profit		138,000
Discount received		3,000
		141,000
Advertising	8,000	
Bank interest	2,000	
Carriage outwards	12,000	
Computing expenses	10,500	
Power	5,000	
Rent	4,000	
Salaries	36,000	
Depreciation	15,000	
Bad debts		
(change in receivables allowance)	(500)	
		(92,000)
Net profit		49,000

A1 Alarms

Statement of financial position at 31 August 20X3

	Cost	Accumulated depreciation	Carrying amount
	$	$	$
ASSETS			
Non-Current assets			
Fixtures	60,000	(30,000)	30,000
Current assets			
Inventories		20,000	
Receivables	30,000		
Allowance for receivables	(1,500)		
		28,500	
Prepayments		2,000	
Bank		2,000	
			52,500
			82,500
CAPITAL AND LIABILITIES			
Capital at 1 September 20X2			20,000
Capital introduced		5,000	
Profit for year		49,000	
Drawings		(33,000)	
			21,000
Capital at 31 August 20X3			41,000
Non-current liability			
Bank loan			20,000
Current liabilities			
Payables		20,000	
Accruals		1,500	
			21,500
			82,500

ORGANISING THE BOOKKEEPING SYSTEM

16   There are 400 units in inventories at the end of the month. These will be all the 300 opening inventories and 100 of the units bought on the 10th. (300 × $10) + (100 × $12) = $4,200

17   *Lower of cost and net realisable value*

	Units	$	$
Small	300	10	3,000
Medium	400	14	5,600
Large	600	16	9,600
			18,200

18   The calculation is as follows:

	$
Opening over draft	(900)
Add cash sales, including sales tax	2,300
Add receipts from customers	7,200
Less payments after discount	(4,750)
Less dishonoured cheques	(400)
Closing balance	3,450

CONTROLLING THE BOOKKEEPING SYSTEM

19   Purchases can be found by constructing a control account:

	$		$
Cash paid	271,150	Opening payables	71,300
Discount received	6,600	Purchases	?
Goods returned	13,750		
Closing payables	68,900		360,400
	360,400		360,400

Purchases = $360,400 – $71,300 = $289,100

20   B

A credit balance on the suspense account indicates that the debit total of the trial balance was higher than the credit total. An error that could cause this would involve whether too great a value having been debited, too little a value have been credited, or a combination of these where an item has been recorded as a debit when it ought to have been a credit.

A   would result in too little having been debited to the customer's account

B   would result in an additional debit entry, therefore this is the correct answer

C   would not cause any imbalance in the trial balance as both the debit and credit entries will have been omitted

D   would not cause any imbalance in the trial balance as both a debit and a credit entry have been made even though they were the wrong way round

21   Sales can be found by constructing a mini sales control account:

	$		$
Receivables at 1.1.03	30,000	Receipts less cash sales	240,000
Sales	?	Receivables at 31.12.03	27,000
	267,000		267,000

Sales = $267,000 – $30,000 = $237,000

INCOMPLETE RECORDS AND INCOME AND EXPENDITURE STATEMENTS

22   COST OF SALES

110%	Sales	6,160
100%	Cost of sales	(?)
	Gross profit	10%

Therefore, cost of sales = 100/110 × 6,160 = $5,600

23   SALES

100%	Sales	??
80%	Cost of sales	(20,000)
	Gross profit	20%

Therefore, sales = 100/80 × 20,000 = $25,000

24 SALES

1331/3%	Sales	??
100%	Cost of sales	(15,000)
	Mark-up	33⅓%

Therefore, sales = 133⅓/100 × 15,000 = $20,000

25 GROSS PROFIT ON SALES

Sales	20,000
Cost of sales	(16,000)
Gross profit	4,000

(a)   Gross profit on sales = 4,000/20,000 × 100 = Margin 20%

(b)   Gross profit on cost of sales = 4,000/16,000 × 100 = Mark-Up 25%

26

PLCA

	$		$
Paid to payables	28,000	Bal b/f	Nil
Bal c/d	16,000	Purchases (bal. fig.)	44,000
	44,000		44,000

RLCA

	$		$
Bal b/f	Nil	Received from receivables	32,000
Sales (bal. fig.)	44,000	Bal c/d	12,000
	44,000		44,000

44,000

Sales	44,000	(which = 30% mark-up on cost)

Less: Opening inventories	Nil	
Add: Purchases	44,000	
Less: Closing inventories (bal. fig.)	(10,154)	
	(33,846)	(use formula: sales = cost x 1.3)
Gross profit	10,154	

27 (i) B

To calculate sales, prepare SLCA.

RLCA

	$		$
Bal b/f	1,000	Received from receivables	18,500
Sales	17,500	Bal c/d	nil
Balancing figure			
	———		———
	18,500		18,500
	———		———

Sales = $17,500

(ii) B

To calculate purchases, prepare PLCA.

PLCA

	$		$
Paid to payables	1,200	Bal b/f	750
Bal c/d	300	Purchases	750
		Balancing figure	
	———		———
	1,500		1,500
	———		———

Purchases = $750

(iii) A

To calculate Gross profit:

	$	$
Sales		17,500
Less: Opening inventories	2,000	
Add: Purchases	750	
	———	
	2,750	
Less: Closing inventories	(500)	
	———	
Cost of goods sold	2,250	(2,250)
	———	———
Gross profit		15,250
		———

(iv) D

Gross profit as % of sales

$$\frac{\text{Gross profit}}{\text{Sales}} \times 100\% = (15,250/17,500) \times 100$$

$$= 87\%$$

(v) A

Gross profit as % of cost of sales

$$\frac{\text{Gross profit}}{\text{Cost of sales}} \times 100 = (15,250/2,250) \times 100$$

$$= 678\%$$

THE MANUFACTURING ACCOUNT

28   Drogba

Income statement for the year ended 31 July 20X1

		$
Sales		450,000
Inventories of finished goods 1 August 20X0	8,000	
Inventories of raw materials at 1 August 20X0	4,000	
Purchases of raw materials	90,000	
Inventories of raw materials at 31 July 20X1	(3,000)	
Cost of raw materials consumed	91,000	
Direct factory wages	60,000	
Prime cost	151,000	
Factory overheads	35,000	
Depreciation charge on factory machinery	35,000	
	221,000	
Work in progress at 1 August 20X0	2,000	
Work in progress at 1 August 20X1	(1,500)	
Production cost of goods completed		221,500
		229,500
Inventories of finished goods 1 August 20X1		(6,000)
Cost of good sold		(223,500)
Gross profit		226,500
Office salaries	50,000	
Depreciation office machinery	15,000	
Advertising	18,000	(83,000)
Net profit		143,500

Drogba

Statement of financial position at 31 July 20X1

ASSETS				$
Non-current assets	*Cost*	*Acc. Depn.*		
Factory machinery	400,000	(90,000)		310,000
Office machinery	200,000	(30,000)		170,000
	600,000	(120,000)		480,000
Current Assets				
Inventories	raw materials		3,000	
	work in progress		1,500	
	finished goods		6,000	
			10,500	
Receivables			40,000	
				50,500
				530,500
CAPITAL AND LIABILITIES				
Capital at 1 August 20X0				337,000
Profit year ended 31 July 20X1			143,500	
Less drawings			(40,000)	103,500
				440,500
Non-current liabilities				
Bank loan				80,000
Current Liabilities				
Bank		3,000		
Payables		7,000		
				10,000
				530,500

THE FINANCIAL STATEMENTS OF LIMITED COMPANIES AND STATEMENT OF CASH FLOWS

29   **Maci plc**

Statement of Comprehensive Income for the Year ended 31 December 20X1

		$000
Sales		1,500
Opening inventories	60	
Purchases	250	
	310	
Closing inventories	(70)	
Cost of sales		(240)
Gross profit		1,260
Administration expenses	380	
Selling and distribution expenses	325	
Depreciation charge	20	
Directors' remuneration	40	
		(765)
Operating profit		495
Debenture interest		(10)
Profit before tax		485
Taxation		(10)
Profit after tax		475
Other operating income		
Gain on property revaluation	75	
Income tax	(20)	
Net gain on property revaluation		55
Total comprehensive income for the period		530

Maci plc

Statement of change in equity for the year ended 31 December 20X1

	Share Capital $000	Revaluation reserve $000	Retained earnings $000	General reserve $000	Total $000
Bal b/f	200		50	25	275
Total comprehensive income		55	475		530
Dividends			(22)		(22)
Transfer			(15)	15	–
Bal c/f	200	55	488	40	783

Statement of Financial Position at 31 December 20X1

ASSETS	$,000	$,000	$,000
Non-current assets	Cost	Depreciation	
Patent	100	–	100
Premises	825	(120)	705
	925	(120)	805

Current Assets		
Inventories		70	
Receivables		110	
			180
			985

EQUITY AND LIABILITIES		
Ordinary shares of $1		200
Revaluation reserve		55
General reserve		40
Retained earnings at 31 December 20X1		488
		783

Non-current liabilities		
Debentures		100	
Income tax on gain		20	
			120

Current liabilities		
Bank		30	
Payables		25	
Debenture interest		5	
Final dividend		12	
Taxation		10	
			82
			985

30   SEAFIELD LTD

Statement of cash flows for the year ended 30 April 20X5

Cash flows from operating activities	$000	$000
Operating profit	987	
Adjustments for		
Depreciation	18	
Profit on sale of non-current assets	(615)	
	─────	
	390	
Increase in receivables	(561)	
Increase in payables	60	
Increase in inventories	(615)	
	─────	
Cash generated from operations	(726)	
(Interest paid)	(117)	
(Tax paid)	(6)	
	─────	(849)
Cash flows from investing activities		
(Purchase of non-current assets)	(159)	
Proceeds on sale of non-current assets	1,212	
	─────	1,053
Cash flows from financing activities		
Proceeds from issue of shares	306	
(Repayment of loans)	(417)	
(Payment of dividends)	(114)	
	─────	(225)
		─────
Net increase in bank and cash		(21)
Bank and cash at the beginning of the period		30
		─────
Bank and cash at the end of the period		9
		─────

Workings

(W1) **Non-current assets**

Cost assets sold	672
Accumulated depreciation	(75)
	─────
Carrying amount	597
Profit on sale — given	615
	─────
Therefore proceeds	1,212
	─────

(W2) **Tax and dividends**

Tax and dividends paid will be the accrued amount in 20X4.

THE INTERPRETATION OF FINANCIAL STATEMENTS

31   (i)   Net profit/sales × 100

          45,000/750,000 × 100 = 6%

   (ii)   Net profit/capital employed X 100

          45,000/400,000 × 100 = 11%

   (iii)   Current assets/current liabilities

          250,000/120,000 = 2.08:1

   (iv)   Quick assets/current liabilities

          100,000/120,000 = 0.83:1

Section 4

ANSWERS TO OBJECTIVE TEST QUESTIONS

THE ACCOUNTING SCENE

1   B, E

2   A

3   D

All of A, B and C are all part of the bookkeeping system. So D is correct.

4   B

5   D

6   D

7   B

8   B

Maintaining ledger accounts, preparing a trial balance and recording transactions are all part of the bookkeeping system.

9   C

10   C

11   D

Management accounts would provide detailed costs and other information regarding manufacturing and trading.

12   A

THE FRAMEWORK OF FINANCIAL STATEMENTS

13   C

14   C

15   C

16   B

17   A

18   B

19   A

		$
Increase in inventories = Increase in working capital		500
Decrease in bank = Decrease in working capital		(800)
Increase in payable = Decrease in working capital		(2,400)
Overall decrease in working capital		(2,700)

20   A

	$
Assets	14,000
Less: Liabilities	(6,250)
	7,750

So a profit of $3,500 increases this to $11,250. The purchase of a non-current asset by cheque and the payment to payables by cheque affects assets and liabilities, but neither affects capital.

21   C

	$
Opening capital	20,000
Introduced	8,000
Drawings	(16,000)
	12,000
Loss – balancing figure	(3,000)
Closing capital	9,000

22   C

23   D

Working backwards often confuses candidates. Try drawing up a short example of an income statement using simple figures of your own, to prove or disprove the options given.

For example:

	$	$
Sales		20,000
Inventories at 31.12.2000	2,000	
Add: Purchases during 2001	8,000	
	10,000	
Less: Inventories at 31.12.2001	(1,000)	
Cost of goods sold		(9,000)
Gross profit		11,000
Less: expenses		4,000
Net profit		7,000

Make all the figures different or you will make mistakes.

You can now see the options A, B and C will not give the correct answer.

24   D

Transactions that affect only assets and liabilities do not affect capital. Therefore, options A, B and C are irrelevant.

Profits increase capital and losses reduce capital.

25 $600

The transactions on credit terms do not affect the cash balance.

26   Increase of $6,150

The effect on working capital is calculated as

	$
Increase in receivables = Increase in working capital	750
Decrease in bank overdraft = Increase in working capital	400
Decrease in payables = Increase in working capital	3,000
Increase in inventories = Increase in working capital	2,000
Overall increase in working capital	6,150

27 **D**

The accounting equation changes when two or more of assets, liabilities or capital changes. Selling goods at a profit would change capital, inventories and receivables; purchasing a non-current asset on credit would change assets and liabilities; the owner withdrawing cash would change assets and capital; receivables paying their accounts in cash would not affect any of these since cash and receivables are both assets.

28 **B**

29 **A**

	$
Sales	24,000
COS (bal fig 2)	(9,600)
Gross profit (bal fig 1)	14,400
Indirect expenses	(12,000)
Net profit (10% x 24,000)	2,400

30 **C**

31 **B**

Note: Closing capital — opening capital — increase in net assets

32 **D**

406,800 + 290,000 + 32,000 – 8,800 = 720,000

33 **D**

The answer is not C because drawings will eventually be transferred to the capital account. The initial entry affects the drawings account.

34 **A**

THE ACCOUNTING SYSTEM IN ACTION

35 **A**

A credit balance in the books of A Ltd indicates that it owes money; none of the distracters would result in a credit balance.

36 **D**

37 **D**

38   **A**

= 1,200 (debit) + 2,100 (debit) − 750 (credit) − 960 (credit) = 1,590 debit

39   **C**

When purchased	*When returned*
Dr Office equipment	Dr Penny
Cr Penny	Cr Office equipment

40   **B**

41   **C**

The inventories account is never used to record purchases.

42   **C**

43   **B**

SUMMARISING THE LEDGER ACCOUNTS

44   **C**

This is a straightforward test of your knowledge of types of errors that can exist. If the wrong account is used, and this results in an incorrect statement of profit, then an error of principle has been made. Debiting the repairs and renewals account results in an extra charge for expenses in the income statement, when the item should be included as a non-current asset on the statement of financial position.

45   **A; C**

Profits: A Decrease

Non-current assets: C No effect

46   **A**

B and D are incorrect as they would give a lower debit side. C is incorrect because it would give a higher credit side.

47   **C**

48   **A**

FURTHER ASPECTS OF LEDGER ACCOUNTS

49   C

A cash discount is a discount for early settlement or prompt payment of an invoice.

50   C

Dr Discount allowed   Cr Receivables

51   B

Income statement

52   A

Dr Supplier   Cr Discount received

53   A

Income statement

54   A

Discount for bulk purchase

55   D

No double entry – the discount is already deducted from the initial amount recorded

56   C

Trading account

57   B

Purchases

58   B

Income statement

59   C

60   D

Discount received is stated in the income statement rather than trading account, therefore the net profit will be affected by $3,000, but the gross profit is not affected.

61   A

$20   ($100 × 20% = $20)

62   B

$16.67   ($100 × 20/120 = $16.67)

63   B

$400

	$
List price	500
Less: Trade discount	(100)
Net purchases	400

64   B

$80

	$
List price	500.00
Less: Trade discount	(100.00)
Net purchases	400.00
Sales tax @ 20%	80.00
	480.00

65   A

		£	£
Dr	Purchases	400	
Dr	Sales tax	80	
Cr	Supplier		480

66   A

Capital employed is increased by making a profit, or by adding more capital. Writing off bad debt would reduce profit; transactions such as C and D merely adjust the split of assets and liabilities but do not add anything overall.

67   C

The year to 31 December 20X3 includes 3/4 of the rent for the year to 30 September 20X3 and 1/4 of the rent for the year to 30 September 20X4, that is:

(3/4 × $600) + (1/4 × $800) = $650

68 $12,000

(8/12 × $18,000) = $12,000

69   D

The change in allowance for receivables is taken to the income statement – an increase is debited and therefore decreases net profit, while a decrease is credited and therefore increases net profit. The resulting balance on the allowance for receivables account is deducted from receivables (current assets), which in turn affects working capital. A decrease in the allowance would increase net profit, and would increase current assets. The latter is not one of the options, therefore D is the answer.

70 B

Sales tax is excluded from sales and purchases accounts, so A and C are incorrect. Sales is a category of revenue, and therefore the sales account is credited.

71

	Hours		$
Gross pay	$20	45	900
Tax		900	
Threshold		(300)	
	20%	600	(120)
Employee SS	8%	900	(72)
Paid to employee			**708**
Wages IS			900
Employer SS	12%	900	108
Income statement charge			**1,008**

72 B

Inventories valuation should take account of trade discounts, but never of cash discounts.

ACCOUNTING FOR NON-CURRENT ASSETS

73 Loss of $1,200

The profit or loss on disposal is the difference between the carrying amount at the time of disposal and the disposal proceeds. An excess of disposal proceeds over carrying amount indicates a profit on disposal, while an excess of carrying amount over disposal proceeds indicates a loss on disposal.

The annual depreciation on the machine is calculated as:

$$\frac{\text{Cost} - \text{residual value}}{\text{Useful economic life}} = \frac{15,000 - 3,000}{4 \text{ years}} = \$3,000 \text{ per year}$$

Non-current asset disposal account

Cost	15,000	Accumulated depreciation	9,000
		Sale proceeds	4,800
		Loss	1,200
	15,000		15,000

74   B

Depreciation never provides a fund for the replacement of the asset, nor does it aim to show assets at their fair values.

75   B

	$
Machine 1: $120,000 × 10%	12,000
Machine 1: $144,000 × 10% × 6/12	7,200
	———
	19,200
	———

76   D

Depreciation is not connected with the putting aside of money for the replacement of the asset, nor does it aim to show assets at their fair values. The charging of depreciation ensures that profits are not overstated.

77   D

Non-current tangible assets should be depreciated over their expected useful life. Answer A would not be appropriate. Assets are rarely valued at their expected selling price – this is discussed in a later chapter. The method of depreciation is irrelevant.

78   B

Cost	300,000
Depreciation 10% 20X5	(30,000)
	———
	270,000
Depreciation 10% 20X6	(27,000)
	———
	243,000
Depreciation 10% 20X7	(24,300)
	———

79   C

Machine 1: Cost 72,000 × 10% = 7,200

Machine 2: Cost 96,000 × 10% = 9,600 × 6/12 = 4,800

Total 7,200 + 4,800 = $12,000

80   D

A, B and C are correct in most situations. Non-purchased goodwill would not be recorded.

81 $44,000

	$
Cost of machine	40,000
Installation	2,500
Training	1,000
Testing	500
	———
	44,000
	———

82 D

ORGANISING THE BOOKKEEPING SYSTEM

83 C

A is incorrect as the journal is one of the books of prime entry in which double-entry rules do apply. B is incorrect as ledger accounts are not maintained in books of prime entry. D is incorrect as subsidiary accounts are ledger accounts that are maintained outside the main ledgers.

84 B

85 $243.90

	$
Stationery	42.30
Travelling cost	76.50
Refreshments	38.70
Sundry payables ($72.00 × 1.2)	86.40
	———
	243.90 to restore to 300
	———

86 $120

The first issues (12 units) would use up the opening inventory of 10 units and 2 units of the purchases at $6 each, leaving 28 units at $6 each. The next issue would be of 8 units, leaving 20 units at $6 each, that is $120.

87   B

The closing inventories figure reduces the cost of goods sold figure, which in turn increases the gross profit.

Therefore, a higher closing inventories figure means a lower cost of goods sold figure, and hence a higher gross profit. In times of rising prices, the FIFO method of inventories valuation will produce higher closing inventories values, and therefore higher gross profit figure.

88 $310

Summarised inventory card

	Quantity	Value ($)	
6 × $30	6	180	
10 × $39.60	10	396	
	16	576	($36 each)
10 × $36	(10)	(360)	
	6	216	
20 × $49	20	980	
	26	1,196	($46 each)
5 × $46	(5)	(230)	
	21	966	

Note: Issues are shown in brackets

Trading account

	$	$
Sales (15 × $60)		900
Opening inventories	180	
Add: Purchases	1,376	
(396 + 980)		
	1,556	
Less: Closing inventories	(966)	
		(590)
Profit		310

89 $4,200

There are 400 units in inventories at the end of the month. These will be all the 300 opening inventories and 100 of the units bought on the 10th. (300 × $10) + (100 × $12) = $4,200

90 $18,200

	Units	$	$
Lower of cost and net realisable value			
Small	300	10	3,000
Medium	400	14	5,600
Large	600	16	9,600
			18,200

91 $3,450 debit

The calculation is as follows:

	$
Opening over draft	(900)
Add cash sales, including sales tax	2,300
Add receipts from customers	7,200
Less payments after discount	(4,750)
Less dishonoured cheques	(400)
Closing balance	3,450

CONTROLLING THE BOOKKEEPING SYSTEM

92   D

93 $8,000 overdrawn

$(6,800) + 300 - (750 \times 2) = (8,000)$

94   D

The nature of the reconciliation indicates that Andrew has an overdraft. For example, unpresented cheques have an adverse effect on the bank balance, here they are increasing therefore the bank account is overdrawn.

95   B

96

	Gross profit	Net profit
Decrease	$3,800	$3,400

97 A

Receivables control

	$		$
Bal b/d	1,950	Cash	96,750
Sales (Balancing figure)	96,000	Bal c/d	1,200
	97,950		97,950

98 A

99 A

Receivables control

	$		$
Bal b/d	300	Cash	2,310
Sales	2,370	Bad debts written off	30
		Discount allowed (bal. fig.)	60
		Bal c/d	270
	2,670		2,670

100 $289,100

Purchases can be found by constructing a control account:

	$		$
Cash paid	271,150	Opening payables	71,300
Discount received	6,600	Purchases	?
Goods returned	13,750		
Closing payables	68,900		
	360,400		360,400

Purchases = $360,400 – $71,300 = $289,100

101 B

A credit balance on the suspense account indicates that the debit total of the trial balance was higher than the credit total. An error that could cause this would involve either too great a value having been debited, too little a value have been credited, or a combination of these where an item has been recorded as a debit when it ought to have been a credit.

A   would result in too little having been debited to the customer's account

B   would result in an additional debit entry, therefore this is the correct answer

C   would not cause any imbalance in the trial balance as both the debit and credit entries will have been omitted

D   would not cause any imbalance in the trial balance as both a debit and a credit entry have been made even though they were the wrong way round

102 $237,000

Sales can be found by constructing a mini sales control account:

	$		$
Receivables at 1.1.03	30,000	Receipts less cash sales	240,000
Sales	?	Receivables at 31.12.03	27,000
	267,000		267,000

Sales = $267,000 – $30,000 = $237,000

103 B

104 C

105 D

106 C

107 A

108 D

109 C

110 A

Omitted from closing inventories, therefore its inclusion will increase profit by the lower of cost and net realisable value, i.e. $100.

111 $2,245 OVERDRAWN

	$
Cash book balance	(2,480)
Unpresented cheques	450
Receipt not yet processed	(140)
Bank charges	(75)
As per statement	(2,245)

112 C

2,125 + 274 – 58 = 2,341

THE REGULATORY FRAMEWORK OF ACCOUNTING

113 B

The accruals convention implies that the profits must be charged with expenses incurred, irrespective of whether or not an invoice has been received.

114 A

Transactions are normally included at their original cost to the business, but that does not preclude reductions in these figures for depreciation and other adjustments, therefore C is incorrect. The accounting professions have attempted to introduce systems of current cost accounting in the past, but these have never replaced the historical cost convention. Accounting transactions are always past transactions but not necessarily using the historical cost convention.

115 D

A is incorrect because assets can be revalued upwards or downwards from their original cost, and depreciated, even under the historical cost convention. B is incorrect as goods should be recorded at the lower of their cost and net realisable value. C is incorrect because profits are calculated without adjustment for the increased cost of replacement inventories, and asset values would be lower than their current value.

116 C

117 D

118 D

119 B

Goodwill arises when more is paid for the net assets of a business than their fair value. Thus, an additional asset is acquired; it is intangible and should be subject to regular impairment reviews to check that the goodwill is not overstated in the statement of financial position.

120 B

121 A

Stewardship is concerned with ensuring that there is a procedure in a place to safeguard assets, provide properly for liabilities, protect against misuse of assets, and report adequately to the shareholders or stakeholders of the organisation.

122 C

123 C

124 D

125 C

126 A

127 B

128 C

129 D

130 D

131 B

132 B

133 C

INCOMPLETE RECORDS AND INCOME AND EXPENDITURE STATEMENTS

134 D

Accumulated fund is equivalent to capital.

135 C

An income and expenditure statement is commonly prepared by a not-for-profit organisation as an alternative to an income statement (as such organisations do not exist to make profits). A summary of cash and bank transactions, and a receipts and payments account are one and the same thing: they both include capital transactions, for example, payments for non-current assets, and neither takes account of accrued and prepaid income or expenses. Thus answers A and B are incorrect. A statement of financial position is a statement of assets, liabilities and capital or accumulated fund.

136 $23,100

Subscription paid			
Bal b/f	1,600	Received	25,000
I&E statement	23,100	Arrears c/f	500
Bal c/f	800		
	25,500		25,500

137 A

Life membership fees represents income in advance and this is credited to a life membership fees account. A proportion of income is transferred to the income and expenditure statement over the assumed life of the membership.

138 D

A receipts and payments account is a summary of the cash and bank transactions.

139

	$
Received in year	62,250
Arrears at beginning	(250)
In advance at beginning	375
In advance at end	(600)
	————
Total to income and expenditure statement	61,775

Subscriptions account (Revenue)

Arrears b/f	250	Prepayment b/f	375
Balancing figure	61,775	Received	62,250
Advance bal c/d	600		
	————		————
	62,625		62,625
	————		————

140 B

Subscription account (Revenue)

Arrears b/d	0	Prepayment b/d	14
Income and expenditure (Balancing figure)	980	Subscription received	1,024
Prepayment c/d	58	Arrears c/d	0
	————		————
	1,038		1,038
	————		————

All arrears income will be credited once received hence ignore both arrears b/d and c/d.

THE MANUFACTURING ACCOUNT

141 $294,000

Cost of goods manufactured is found as follows:

	$
Opening inventories of raw materials	20,000
Purchases of raw materials	100,000
Less: Closing inventories of raw materials	(22,000)
	98,000
Direct wages	80,000
Prime cost	178,000
Production overheads	120,000
	298,000
Less: Increase in work-in-progress	(4,000)
Cost of goods manufactured	294,000

142   D

A decrease in work-in-progress means fewer goods are partly complete, thus the value of completed goods will be higher.

143   C

Royalties paid on production are a direct expense and are therefore part of prime cost.

144   D

145   B

The cost of an extension to a factory is a capital expenditure and would be shown as an asset in the statement of financial position.

THE FINANCIAL STATEMENTS OF LIMITED COMPANIES AND STATEMENT OF CASH FLOWS

146 A

Revenue reserves can be distributed as dividends, so B is incorrect. Revenue reserves are not set aside to replace revenue items; they could be set aside for a specific purpose but this is only one use of revenue reserves.

147

	Debit	Credit
Bank	640,000	
Share premium		240,000
Share capital		400,000

148 A

Dividends proposed are not shown in the statement of changes in equity. Directors' and auditors' fees are normal business expenses and appear in the statement of comprehensive income.

149 C

	$
Profit	4,000
Add back depreciation	6,000
	———
Net cash inflow	10,000
Purchase of non-current assets	(12,500)
	———
Decrease	(2,500)

150 D

A company does not have a single capital account – its capital consists of shares and reserves. The statement of comprehensive income shows how a profit is earned, not how it is allocated. A reserve account will only show what profit has been allocated to it, not how the total profit has been allocated.

151 D

A and B are both forms of revenue reserve. Issuing shares at a premium increases reserves, but they are capital reserves anyway.

152 A

All the others are part of the equity capital.

153 D

154 C

Gains on revaluation of property. These are shown net of tax.

155 C & E

Both of these items are in a comprehensive income statement.

156 D

157 B

158 A

	$
Charge for 20X7	2,700
Over provision 20X6 (2,400 – 2,200)	(200)
	2,500

159 C

160 D

A transfer of shares has no effect on the company's share capital.

161 D

Share premium is a capital reserve created when shares are issued at a price above their nominal value.

162 A

Proposed dividends do not appear in financial statements because they are not recognised as a liability until they are approved; declared dividends do appear because they are a liability; directors do not have to propose a dividend to the shareholders, even if there are available profits; dividends may be paid just once in a year.

163 D

164 C

165 B

THE INTERPRETATION OF FINANCIAL STATEMENTS

166 $500

		$
Selling price (SP)	140	700
Cost of sales (COS)	100	???
		___
Gross profit	40	???
		___

Cost of sales = 700 x 100/140 = $500

167 7.5 times

Rate of inventories turnover is found by dividing cost of goods sold by average inventory. Average inventory is

$$\left(\frac{24,000 + 20,000}{2} \right) = \$22,000$$

$$\text{Inventory turnover} = \frac{\text{Cost of sales}}{\text{Average inventory}}$$

	£
Opening inventory	24,000
Purchases	160,000
	_____
	184,000
Less: Closing inventory	(20,000)
	_____
Cost of goods sold	164,000
	_____

Rate of inventory turnover is therefore 164,000/22,000 = 7.5 times

168 D

You need only know the correct formula here.

169 A

The gearing ratio is the proportion of long-term loans to shareholders' funds, thus it follows that if a decrease in long-term loans is less than a decrease in the shareholders' funds, the gearing ratio will rise.

170

The current ratio is current assets: current liabilities, that is 5,800:2,200 = 2.6:1. The quick ratio is current assets minus inventory: current liabilities, that is 2,000:2,200 = 0.9:1.

171 D

Transfers between revenue reserves, as mentioned in A and B, have no effect on the overall total of revenue reserves; issuing shares at a premium increases capital reserves; the paying of dividends must be from revenue reserves, so these will decrease.

172 D

	$
Opening inventories	9,075
Add: Purchases	36,325
	45,400
Less: Closing inventories	(4,500)
Cost of sales	40,900

	%		
Gross profit margin	100	Sales	
Balancing figure	(70)	(Cost of sales)	40,900
Given	30	Gross profit	

Gross profit = 30/70 × 40,900 = $17,529

173 C

44,000/324,500 × 365 days = 49 days

Average inventories / COS x 365

Average inventories = (50,000 + 38,000)/2 = 44,000

174 A

60,000/430,000 × 365 days = 51 days

Trade receivables/Sales × 365

175 B

40,000/312,500 × 365 days = 47 days

Trade payables/Purchases × 365

176 B

108,000/56,000 = 1.93:1

Current assets: Current liabilities

Current assets = Trade receivables 60,000 + Prepayments 4,000 + Cash in hand 6,000 + Closing inventories 38,000 = 108,000

Current liabilities = Bank overdraft 8,000 + Trade payables 40,000 + Accruals 3,000 + Declared dividends 5,000 = 56,000

177 A

(108,000 – 38,000)/56,000 = 1.25:1

(Current assets — Inventories) : Current liabilities

Current assets and liabilities as above

178 C

Cash cycle = Inventories days + Receivables days — Payables days = 49 + 51-47 (as per answers above) = 53 days

179 D

$32,000/0.4 = $80,000

Current ratio is 1.4:1 and

Current assets — Current liabilities = 32,000

If Current liabilities are A then Current assets are 1.4A

1.4A – A = 32,000; 0.4A = 32,000

Hence A = 32,000/0.4 = Current liabilities

180 C

Current liabilities = $80,000; Current assets = $80,000 × 1.4 = $112,000

Quick assets = $80,000 × 0.9 = $72,000

Therefore, inventories will be the difference between current assets and quick assets ($112,000 – 72,000) = $40,000

181 D

Cost of sales = $40,000 × 8.775 = $351,000; Gross profit is 25% of sales

Therefore, sales equals to $351,000/0.75 = $468,000

182   A

Closing receivables = $468,000 × 6/52 = $54,000

Current assets = $112,000 (see answer 180)

Closing inventories = $40,000 (see answer 180)

Bank balance = $112,000 − $54,000 − $40,000 = $18,000

Section 5

MOCK ASSESSMENT 1

1   Which of the following items should be classified as capital expenditure?

A   Repairs to motor vans

B   Depreciation of machinery

C   Extension of premises

D   Purchase of motor vans for resale

2   Match the following users with their information requirements:

	Users		Requirements
1	The public	A	The ability of the company to continue, and to pay pensions in the future
2	The government	B	The use of information for taking operational decisions in running the company
3	Employees	C	The policies of a company and how those policies affect the community, for example health and safety
4	Internal users	D	The performance and financial position of a company and its ability to pay dividends
5	Shareholders	E	The ability of a company to pay taxes, and administer other taxes, for example value-added tax

3   The management accounts within a limited company are determined by

A   company law

B   company law and international accounting standards

C   the shareholders

D   directors

4   The accounting convention that, in times of rising prices, tends to understate asset values and overstate profits, is the

A   going concern convention

B   prudence convention

C   realisation convention

D   historical cost convention

5 Recording the purchase of computer stationery by debiting the computer equipment account would result in

    A   an overstatement of profit and an overstatement of non-current assets

    B   an understatement of profit and an overstatement of non-current assets

    C   an overstatement of profit and an understatement of non-current assets

    D   an understatement of profit and an understatement of non-current assets

6 What does 'Limited' mean in a company's name?

    A   A company's liability is limited to the total amount of its authorised share capital

    B   A company's liability is limited to the total amount of its issued share capital

    C   The members' liability is limited to the total amount paid or payable on the shares held by them

    D   The members' liability is limited to the nominal value of the shares held by them

7 What is the core objective of accounting?

    A   To provide financial information to the users of such information

    B   To maintain records of assets and liabilities

    C   To keep a record of transactions

    D   To fulfil statutory requirements

8 Which of the following is not a qualitative characteristic of financial statements?

    A   Relevance

    B   Comparability

    C   Profitability

    D   Understandability

9 Sharon started a business on 1 January 20X1 with $30,000 capital. During the year 20X1 she drew $15,000 out of the business and paid in a legacy of $9,000 from her uncle. At 31 December 20X1 the business's net assets were valued at $54,000.

What was the business's profit for the year?

    A $15,000

    B $24,000

    C $30,000

    D $39,000

10 An imprest system is designed to help reconcile the cash book with the bank statement.

True/false

11   The following information is available about a company's receivables:

	$
Balance b/f at 1 January 20X3	166,200
Allowance for receivables at 1 January 20X3	13,320
Increase in provision during 20X3	1,440
Discount allowed in year	47,280
Sales in year	1,460,760
Contra purchase ledger in year	106,800
Receipts from customers in year	1,370,400

The balance carried forward at 31 December 20X3 on the sales ledger control account is
$ _____

12   Job purchases goods on credit from Sad Limited for $24,000. What is the correct double entry?

	Debit	*Credit*
A	Purchase	Receivables
B	Purchases	Payables
C	Payables	Purchases
D	Payables	Cash

13   Alpha's business owed $60 to trade payables at 1 July 20X4 and $90 at 30 June 20X5. Purchases on credit amounted to $3,000 during the year and suppliers allowed a total of $150 cash discount.

How much was paid to payables during the year?

A $2,760

B $2,820

C $2,880

D $2,940

14   Red operates the imprest system for petty cash. At 1 March there was a float of $200, but it was decided to increase this to $250 at the end of March. During March, the petty cashier received $40 from a member of staff who had claimed excessive expenses in a previous month. The cashier then paid $75 for drinks and biscuits, $72 for stationery and $40 for window cleaning. What was drawn from the bank account for petty cash at the end of March?

A $147

B $187

C $197

D $237

15 Assuming that it reconciles with the cash book, how would a balance marked 'Cr' on a business's bank statement appear in its statement of financial position?

  A Current asset

  B Current liability

  C Non-current asset

  D Non-current liability

16 A purchase day book total $7,390 had been entered in the control account as $7,930. What will the impact of the required correction be?

	Control account	List of balances
A	Debit $540	No effect
B	Debit $540	Decrease total by $540
C	Credit $540	No effect
D	Debit $1,080	No effect

17 A company's cash book shows a debit balance of $8,400. The bank statement as at the same date shows an overdrawn balance of $2,520. Which one of the following timing differences could account for the discrepancy?

  A Cheques drawn but not yet presented amounted to $5,880

  B Cheques received but not yet cleared amounted to $5,880

  C Cheques drawn but not yet presented amounted to $10,920

  D Cheques received but not yet cleared amounted to $10,920

18 Which of the following errors would not cause there to be a difference in the trial balance?

  A incomplete double entry

  B addition error

  C transaction not recorded at all

  D transposition error in the debit entry

19 Which one of the following attributes is the most important for any code to possess in order to be of use in an accounting system?

  A Combination of letters and digits to ensure input accuracy

  B Completeness of numbering

  C Each code is a unique number

  D Easy to amend

20   **Grey paid $3,600 insurance during the year to 31 March 20X1.**

As at 1 April 20X0 he had overpaid $1,200, and the correct charge in the income statement for year to 31 March 20X1 is $3,900. What is the amount of the prepayment at 31 March 20X1?

A $600

B $900

C $105

D $1,200

21   **Businesses charge depreciation on non-current assets in order to**

A   ensure that sufficient funds are available to replace the assets

B   spread the cost of the assets over their estimated useful life

C   comply with the prudence convention

D   reduce profits and dividends

22   **A company buys a car for $60,000 and expects it to have a useful life of 5 years. It depreciates the car at 50% reducing balance and sells it after 3 years for $30,000. The profit of disposal is $ _____**

23   **Graham has the following balances in his trial balance at 31 December 20X3.**

	$
Total receivables	420,000
Irrecoverable debts written off (no previous allowance)	3,000
Allowance for receivables at 1 January 20X3	30,000

The company wishes to carry forward an allowance for receivables equal to 10% of total receivables.

What is the total effect of the above on the income statement for the year ended 31 December 20X3?

A   charge of $14,700

B   credit of $14,700

C   charge of $15,000

D   credit of $15,000

24   **Under what heading should debentures be shown in a company's statement of financial position?**

A   equity

B   current assets

C   current liabilities

D   non-current liabilities

25   Kiren sells three products X, Y and Z. At the company's year end the inventories held are as follows:

	Cost	Selling price
	$	$
X	3,600	4,500
Y	18,600	18,300
Z	2,760	2,790

At sale a 5% commission is payable by the company to its agent. What is the total amount of these inventories in the company's financial statements?

A $23,636

B $24,282

C $24,960

D $25,635

26   Alan's business made purchases of $54,000 during the month of January 20X6. His inventories were $6,000 on 1 January and $12,000 on 31 January. His gross profit margin is 25% of sales.

What were his sales for the month?

A $60,000

B $64,000

C $75,000

D $80,000

27   A company sold goods with a net value of $200,000 and made purchases with a gross amount of $162,000. The rate of VAT was 20%. The difference between VAT output tax and VAT input tax is?

A $933

B $6,333

C $7,600

D $13,000

28   Hello Limited sold a motor van which it had purchased three years ago for $24,000 and which it had depreciated each year at 50% by the reducing balance method.

The company traded this van in for a new one costing $36,000, and paid the supplying garage $34,400 by cheque.

What was the profit or loss on the sale of the old van?

A $1,400 loss

B $1,600 profit

C $3,000 profit

D $3,000 loss

29   **Euripides is a landlord with two tenants, Medea and Orestes. He prepares his financial statements for the year ended 31 December 20X6.**

The following information is available:

	Medea	Orestes
	$	$
Rent paid in advance 31.12.X5	1,000	
Rent owed 31.12.X5		1,400
Rent paid during year	4,000	5,000
Rent paid in advance at 31.12.X6		500
Rent owed at 31.12.X6	200	

What figure for rental income will appear in Euripides's income statement?

A $8,300

B $8,900

C $9,100

D $9,700

30   **Bow Ltd's year end is 31 December. For various reasons, inventories could not be counted this year until 6 January. The inventories amount at this date was $445,800. Detailed records were kept of inventories movements between the year end and the physical inventory count. The following figures (all stated at cost) are available:**

	$
Sales	7,500
Purchases	6,930
Returns inwards	1,650
Returns outwards	840

The amount of inventories in Bow Ltd's statement of financial position at 31 December is $ _____

31   **Mr Malopa has paid rent of $14,400 for the period 1 January 20X4 to 31 December 20X4. His accounts drawn up for nine months up to 30 September 20X4 should show the rent expense as:**

A   Only a rent expense of $7,200

B   A rent expense of $10,800 and a prepayment of $3,600

C   A rent expense of $10,800 and accrued revenue of $3,600

D   A rent expense of $14,400 with an explanatory note that this is the usual charge for twelve months

32 Atomic Ltd purchases a machine for which the supplier's list price is $162,000. Atomic pays $117,000 in cash and trades in an old machine which has a carrying amount of $72,000. It is the company's policy to depreciate such machines at the rate of 10% per annum on cost.

What is the carrying amount of the machine after one year?

A $105,300

B $145,800

C $170,100

D $172,800

33 The difference between an income statement and an income and expenditure statement is that

A   an income and expenditure statement is an alternative international term for an income statement

B   an income statement prepared for a business and an income and expenditure statement is prepared for a non-profit-making organisation

C   an income statement is prepared on an accruals basis and an income and expenditure account is prepared on a cash flow basis

D   an income statement is prepared for a manufacturing business and an income and expenditure statement is prepared for a non-manufacturing business

34 The following information is given for the year ended 31 October 20X0:

	$
Purchase of raw materials	28,000
Returns inwards	2,000
Increase in inventories of raw materials	850
Direct wages	10,500
Carriage inwards	1,250
Production overheads	7,000
Decrease in work-in-progress	2,500

The value of factory cost of goods completed is $ ....

35 Which one of the following costs would be included in the calculation of prime cost in a manufacturing account?

A   Cost of transporting raw materials from suppliers premises

B   Wages of factory workers engaged in machine maintenance

C   Depreciation of lorries used for deliveries to customers

D   Cost of indirect production materials

36   Ferry's inventories on 1 January 20X4 cost $14,300 and his payables were $3,750. During the year his sales amounted to $174,000, earning an average mark-up of 33% on cost. He paid $133,650 to suppliers during the year and payables' balances at 31 December 20X4 totalled $4,900. On the same date his shop was burgled and all his inventories were stolen.

What was the cost of the stolen inventories?

A $16,300

B $18,273

C $30,800

D $33,100

37   **The reducing-balance method of depreciating non-current assets is more appropriate than the straight-line method when**

A   there is no expected residual value for the asset

B   the expected life of the asset is not capable of being estimated

C   the asset is expected to be replaced in a short period of time

D   it more accurately reflects the consumption of the asset

38   **Which of the following items should be classified as revenue expenditure?**

A   Drawings of goods for private consumption

B   Petrol for proprietor's wife's private car

C   Purchase of a new word processor

D   Purchase of an ink cartridge for word processor

39   **A business has opening inventories of $24,000 and closing inventories of $36,000. Purchase returns were $10,000. The cost of goods sold was $222,000. Purchases were $ _____**

40   **The stewardship function is carried out by**

A   the internal auditors

B   the external auditors

C   the treasurer of a not-for-profit organisation

D   the management of an organisation

41   **The main objective of the internal audit function is to provide support to the external auditor, therefore reducing the cost of the external audit.**

True/false

42 Claim Limited paid $20,400 cash for electricity during the year ended 31 December 20X3. At 1 January 20X3 the company owed $15,000 and at 31 December 20X3 it owed $17,400.

What charge for electricity should appear in the company's income statement for the year ended 31 December 20X3?

A $17,400

B $18,000

C $20,400

D $22,800

43 What action does a company need to take when discovering that a major customer has gone bankrupt? An allowance for this receivable had been made earlier in the year. The entries now required are

A   Dr Irrecoverable debts   Cr Receivables

B   Dr Receivables   Cr Irrecoverable debts

C   Dr Receivables   Cr Allowance for receivables

D   Dr Allowance for receivables   Cr Receivables

44 Ensuring that the assets of a company are properly safeguarded and utilised efficiently and effectively as part of

A   the stewardship function exercised by the directors

B   the external auditor's responsibility

C   the function of the financial accountant

D   the internal auditor's responsibility

45 A computerised spreadsheet package is most suitable for

A   recording the dual aspect of accounting transactions

B   maintaining an audit trail of transactions

C   performing bank reconciliations

D   preparing a cash budget

46 XYZ's plant and machinery had a carrying value of $450,000 at the year end. Its opening balance was $325,000. During the year depreciation of $63,000 was charged and an asset with a carrying value of $12,000 was disposed of resulting in a profit on disposal of $3,000. What it the cash outflow for purchases of plant and machinery in the year?

A $176,000

B $197,000

C $200,000

D $203,000

47 **Candy returned some goods to a supplier because they were faulty. The original purchase price of these goods was $24,780.**

The ledger clerk treated the return correctly on both the payables' ledger control account and the individual payables' account, but debited the purchase returns account with $25,860.

What is the correcting entry which needs to be made?

	Debit	$	Credit	$
A	Suspense account	1,080	Purchase returns	1,080
B	Purchase returns	1,080	Suspense account	1,080
C	Suspense account	50,640	Purchase returns	50,640
D	Purchase returns	50,640	Suspense account	50,640

48 **A business has the following trading account for the year ending 31 May 2008:**

	£	£
Sales revenue		90,000
Opening inventory	8,000	
Add: Purchases	53,000	
	61,000	
Less: Closing inventory	(12,000)	
		(49,000)
Gross profit		41,000

Its rate of inventory turnover for the year is

………………. times (to 1 decimal place)

49 **A 'fair presentation' or 'true and fair view' is one that**

A   presents the financial statements in such a way as to exclude errors that would affect the actions of those reading them

B   occurs when the financial statements have been audited

C   shows the financial statements of an organisation in an understandable format

D   shows the assets on the statement of financial position at their fair value

50 **Which of the following statements is not correct?**

A   Internal auditors may review value for money

B   Internal auditors should not liaise with external auditors

C   Internal audit is part of internal control

D   Internal audit should be independent of the activities it audits

Section 6

MOCK ASSESSMENT 2

1   **Which of the following best explains, what is meant by 'capital expenditure'? Capital expenditure is the expenditure**

    A   on non-current assets, including repairs and maintenance

    B   on expensive assets

    C   relating to the issue of share capital

    D   relating to the acquisition or improvement of non-current assets

2   **In times of rising prices, the historical cost convention results in**

    A   inventories being valued at cost price if this is higher than their net realisable value

    B   non-current assets being valued at their original cost, with no adjustment for depreciation

    C   profits being overstated and statement of financial position values being understated

    D   profits being understated and statement of financial position values being overstated

3   **Which one of the following does not explain the distinction between financial accounts and management accounts?**

    A   Financial accounts are more accurate than management accounts

    B   Financial accounts are usually produced annually and management accounts are usually produced monthly

    C   Financial accounts are regulated, management accounts are not regulated

    D   Financial accounts are audited by the internal auditors, management accounts are audited by the external auditors

4   **If the owner of a business takes goods from inventories for his own personal use, the accounting convention to be considered is the**

    A   prudence convention

    B   materiality convention

    C   money measurement convention

    D   separate entity convention

5   During the year ended 31 December 20X2 the net assets of Sharon's business increased from $54,000 to $63,000. She drew $18,000 out of the business and paid in a football pools win of $36,000.

What was the profit or loss for the year?

A $9,000 profit

B $9,000 loss

C $27,000 profit

D $27,000 loss

6   The stewardship function requires directors to safeguard the assets of the business on behalf of its shareholders.

True/false

7   Which of the following is not a reason for providing depreciation on tangible non- current asset?

A   They have a limited useful life

B   They are part of the cost of generating the revenue for a period, and that cost should be matched with the revenue

C   The cost of the asset is consumed over its life and hence the statement of financial position should reflect this consumption

D   It is a means of valuing an asset

8   Which one of the following gives the best definition of bookkeeping?

A   To calculate the distributable profit for the year

B   To record, categorise and summarise financial transactions

C   To help users with their decision making

D   To calculate the taxation due to the government

9   The objective of financial statements is to provide management with information useful for decision making.

True/false

10   Sam returned goods to Dane which he had bought on credit from her. What is the double entry necessary to record this transaction in the books of Dane?

	Debit	Credit
A	Sales returns	Cash
B	Sales returns	Receivables
C	Cash	Sales returns
D	Cash	Receivables

11 Faulty goods, which had cost $2,400, had been returned to a supplier, but the return had not been recorded in the books. What will the impact of the required correction be?

	Control account	List of balances
A	No effect	Decrease total by $2,400
B	Debit $2,400	No effect
C	Debit $2,400	Decrease total by $2,400
D	No effect	No effect

12 A company's bank statement shows an overdraft of $3,204 at 31 March 20X4. The statement includes bank charges of $46 which have not yet been recorded in the company's cash book. The statement does not include cheques for $780 paid to suppliers, nor an amount of $370 received from a receivable; both of these amounts appear in the bank statement for April 2004.

If the company prepares a statement of financial position as at 31 March 20X4, the figure for bank overdraft should be

A $2,748

B $2,794

C $3,568

D $3,614

13 Which of the following errors would cause there to be a difference in the trial balance?

A amount posted to the wrong account

B transaction correctly posted but with the incorrect amount in both accounts

C transaction entered on the debit side of both accounts

D transaction not recorded at all

14 The cost of an inventory item held by a company is $80 and its net realisable value is $70. When preparing the statement of financial position, the accountant of the company wants to know the basis of valuation of such inventory item. Which of the following conventions should dictate his choice?

A the going concern convention

B the money measurement convention

C the prudence convention

D the accruals convention

15 Your firm's bank statement at 31 October 20X8 shows a balance of $26,800. You subsequently discover that the bank has dishonoured a customer's cheque for $600 and has charged bank charges of $100, neither of which is recorded in your cash book. There are unrepresented cheques totalling $2,800. You further discover that an automatic receipt from a customer of $390 has been recorded as a credit in your cash book.

Your cash book balance, prior to correcting the errors and omissions, was $ _____

16   The cost of inventories shown in the statement of financial position at 31 March 20X2 of Kelly stated on the LIFO basis were $25,500. Had the inventories been stated on a FIFO basis they would have been $27,600. The effect of adopting the FIFO basis on the financial statements for the year ended 31 March 20X2 would be to

A   reduce profit and increase working capital $2,100

B   increase net assets and increase profits by $2,100

C   reduce shareholders' funds and increase current assets by $2,100

D   increase current assets and increases losses by $2,100

17   The following information relates to the business of Andy for the year ended 31 December 20X2.

	$
Opening receivables	2,000
Opening payables	1,800
Discounts received	20
Cash sales	500
Cash from customers (including $200 from a customer whose debt was written off in 20X1)	9,500
Credit purchases	6,000
Receivables to be written off	200
Discounts allowed	30
Returns inwards	40
Amounts paid to suppliers	5,400
Returns outwards	50
Credit sales	13,000
Allowance for receivables (in addition to those written off)	150

What is the closing balance of the sales ledger control account?

A $4,930

B $5,230

C $5,280

D $5,430

18   The following information related to a company's rent and local business tax account:

	Closing balance	Opening balance
Local business tax prepayment	90	60
Rent accrual	360	300

Cash payments of $2,520 were made in respect of rent and local business tax during the period. The charge to the income statement for the year is

A $2,550

B $2,490

C $2,110

D $3,030

19   Your purchase ledger control account has a balance at 1 October 20X8 of $69,000 credit. During October, credit purchases were $156,800, cash purchases were $4,800, and payments made to suppliers, excluding cash purchases and after deducting cash discounts of $2,400, were $137,800. Purchase returns were $9,400. What was the closing balance on the control account?

20   A business operates the imprest system for petty cash. At 1 December there was a float of $150, but it was decided to increase this to $180 from 1 January onwards. During December, the petty cashier received $15 from staff for personal use of the photocopier and a cheque for $40 was cashed for an employee. In December, cheques were drawn for $300 for petty cash. What was the total expense paid from petty cash in December?

A $215

B $245

C $295

D $305

21   What could be the reason for a difference between the purchase ledger control account and the total of payable's balances?

A   Incorrect calculation of a trade discount

B   Omission of cheque payment to a supplier from ledgers

C   The total of cash receipts in the cash book was miscast

D   Returns outwards were not entered in the personal account of the supplier

22   A business buys a machine for $60,000 and depreciates it at 10% per annum by the reducing instalment method. What is the depreciation charge for the second year of the machine's use?

A $4,800

B $4,860

C $5,400

D $6,000

23   A business sells a van on 31 December 20X3 which it bought on 1 January 20X1 for $18,000 and has depreciated each year at 25% per annum by the straight line method. It trades this van in for a new one costing $30,000, and pays the supplier $27,600 by cheque. What is the profit or loss on disposal?

A $2,100 loss

B $2,400 profit

C $4,500 profit

D $4,500 loss

24   **Which of the following items is shown in a receipts and payments account but not in an income and expenditure statement?**

A   The clubhouse electricity bill

B   Subscriptions

C   Affiliation fees

D   The purchase of minibus

25   **Brain Ltd owns property which cost $468,000 to acquire (being $138,000 for the land and $330,000 for the buildings). The company's accounting policy is to depreciate buildings (but not land) at the rate of 2% per annum.**

After three years, what will be the carrying amount of the asset 'land and buildings' in the company's books?

A $307,200

B $439,920

C $448,200

D $459,420

26   **Ash started a business on 1 October 20X7. The following information is available for the year ended 30 September 20X8:**

Cash received from customers	$60,450
Cash paid to suppliers	$63,360
Trade receivables at 30 September 20X8	$17,880
Trade payables at 30 September 20X8	$7,020
Mark-up on cost	40%

What is the cost of inventories at 30 September 20X8?

A $14,430

B $20,181

C $23,382

D $27,090

27   **At 1 January 2004 the ledger accounts of a trader show accrued rent payable of $1,500. During the year he pays rent bills totalling $7,650, including one bill for $2,250 in respect of the quarter ending 31 January 2005.**

What is the income statement charge for rent payable for the year ended 31 December 2004?

A $5,400

B $6,900

C $8,400

D $9,900

28   Which one of the following costs would be included in the calculation of prime cost in a manufacturing account?

    A   Factory premises repairs

    B   Office wages

    C   Direct production wages

    D   Depreciation on machinery

29   A company's usage of raw materials during a year was $35,800. Direct labour costs amounted to $53,400, production overheads to $14,800 and administration overheads to $10,200. Opening work-in-progress was $3,600 and closing work-in-progress was $4,700.

In the company's manufacturing account, factory cost of finished goods produced is

    A $102,900

    B $105,000

    C $113,100

    D $115,300

30   What is an imprest system?

    A   Part of a computerised accounting system

    B   Helps to perform control account reconciliations

    C   Records the use of a company's seal

    D   Helps to control petty cash

31   Which one of the following does not form part of a limited company's equity capital?

    A   Ordinary share capital

    B   Debentures

    C   Revaluation reserve

    D   Debenture redemption reserve

32   United Ltd purchases a company car for $198,000 plus sales tax at 20%. The car is expected to have a life of three years and a residual value of $90,000. Payment is made partly in cash and partly by trading in an old car with a carrying amount of $70,560 and a trade-in value of $54,000. The company uses the straight-line basis to depreciate its cars. What is the carrying amount of the car after one year, assuming that the sales tax is irrecoverable?

    A $140,000

    B $162,000

    C $173,040

    D $188,400

33   A club takes credit for subscriptions when they become due. On 1 January 20X5 arrears of subscriptions amounted to $38 and subscriptions paid in advance were $72. On 31 December 20X5 the amounts were $48 and $80, respectively. Subscription receipts during the year were $790.

In the income and expenditure statements for 20X5 the income from subscriptions would be shown as:

A $748

B $788

C $790

D $792

34   An increase in the allowance for receivables would result in

A   a decrease in working capital

B   an increase in working capital

C   an increase in liabilities

D   an increase in profit

35   Which of the following would cause a change in the proprietor's funds of a sole trader?

A   Depreciation of a non-current asset

B   Purchase of a non-current asset for cash

C   Purchase of a non-current asset on credit

D   Sale of a non-current asset at carrying amount

36   Your organisation uses the weighted average cost method of valuing inventories. During September 20X0, the following inventories details were recorded.

Opening balance	60 units valued at $4 each
6 September	Purchase of 100 units at $4.80 each
9 September	Sale of 80 units
12 September	Purchase of 120 units at $5 each
23 September	Sale of 50 units

The value of the inventories at 30 September 20X0 was $ _____

37   The gross profit mark-up on cost is 60 per cent where sales are $120,000 and

A   cost of sales is $48,000

B   gross profit is $72,000

C   gross profit is $75,000

D   cost of sales is $75,000

38 A cash payment to Robert Conquests Limited of $6,000 had been credited to Norman Cross Limited's account in the Payables' ledger. What will the impact of the required correction be?

	Control account	*List of balances*
A	No effect	No effect
B	No effect	Decrease total by $6,000
C	No effect	Decrease total by $12,000
D	Debit $12,000	Decrease total by $12,000

39 STU paid $5,600 insurance in the year ended 31 August 20X3. At 1 September 20X2 it had over paid $1,000 and a correct income statement charge for the year ended 31 August 20X3 is $5,800. What is the amount of the prepayment at 31 August 20X3?

A $200

B $800

C $1,000

D $1,200

40 Your firm has the following manufacturing figures:

	$
Prime cost	112,000
Factory overheads	9,000
Opening work-in-progress	12,400
Factory cost of goods completed	114,000

Closing work-in-progress is $ _____

41 LMN paid $320,000 in net wages to its employees in June. Employees' tax was $30,000, employees' national insurance was $18,000 and employer's national insurance was $22,000. What is the amount of the wages expense to be charged in the income statement for the month of June?

A $294,000

B $342,000

C $368,000

D $390,000

42 A company's receivable days (based on average receivables) at 31 October 20X8 is 45 days. Its sales for the year are $3,253,680 and its receivables at 31 October 20X7 were $368,125. What is the balance on receivables at 31 October 20X8 (to the nearest $ and assuming a 365 day year)?

A $384,632

B $401,139

C $404,040

D $434,153

43 The operating profit for the year ended 30 September 20X6 of CD was $780,000. This was after charging depreciation of $45,000. Extracts from the statements of financial position of CD were as follows:

	30 Sept X6	30 Sept X5
	$000	$000
Inventory	56	43
Receivables	32	55
Payables	57	62

The cash generated from operations of CD for the year was $ _____.

44 FGH's current ratio is 2.1:1 and its quick (acid test) ratio is 1.6:1. Its current liabilities are $425,000.

The carrying value of inventory was $ _____.

45 Extracts from PQR's statements of financial position are:

	30 Nov X1	30 Nov X0
	$000	$000
Share capital	150	50
Loans	300	500

The company paid a dividend of $55,000 to shareholders during the year.

What is the net cash-flow from financing activities?

A $45,000 outflow

B $155,000 outflow

C $355,000 outflow

D $245,000 inflow

46 The responsibility for ensuring that all accounting transactions are properly recorded and summarised in the final financial statements lies with

A   the external auditors

B   the internal auditors

C   the shareholders

D   the directors

47 The main purpose of an external audit is to

A   detect errors and fraud

B   ensure that the financial statements are accurate

C   determine that the financial statements show a true and fair view of the financial state of the organisation

D   ensure that all transactions have been recorded in the books of account

48 A computerised accounts package would be most useful in maintaining

A   the ledger accounts

B   the books of prime entry

C   a register of non-current assets

D   the inventories records

49 There is only one true and fair presentation of a company's financial statements.

True/false

50 Which one of the following best describes the role of the internal auditor?

A   Ensuring value for money

B   Reporting to management on the internal control system

C   Auditing the financial statements

D   Detecting fraud

Section 7

ANSWERS TO MOCK ASSESSMENT 1

1   C

2   1C, 2E, 3A, 4B, 5D

3   D

4   D

5   A

6   C

7   A

8   C

9   C

Initial capital — drawings + further capital introduced (legacy) +/− profit/(loss) = Closing capital (net assets)

30,000 − 15,000 + 9,000 +/− profit/(loss) = 54,000

Therefore profit = 54,000 − 30,000 + 15,000 − 9,000 = 30,000

10   **False**

The imprest system helps to control petty cash, not the bank account.

11   **$102,480**

	SLCA		
Bal b/f	166,200	Discount allowed	47,280
Sales	1,460,760	Contra purchase ledger	106,800
		Receipts from receivables	1,370,400
		Bal c/d (bal fig)	102,480
	1,626,960		1,626,960

12   B

13   B

Payables

	$		$
Discount received	150	Bal b/d	60
Cash (bal. fig.)	2,820	Purchases	3,000
Bal c/d	90		
	———		———
	3,060		3,060
	———		———

14   C

	$
Opening petty cash float	200
Received from member of staff	40
Paid out in expenses	
(75 + 72 + 40)	(187)
	———
	53
From bank account (bal fig)	197
	———
Required closing cash float	250
	———

15   A

16   A

17   D

Cheques received were lodged into the bank but were not yet cleared.

18   C

19   C

20   B

Insurance

	$		$
Bal b/d	1,200	Income statement	3,900
Cash	3,600	Bal c/d	900
	———		———
	4,800		4,800
	———		———

21   **B**

22   **$22,500**

	$
Cost	60,000
Depreciation year 1: $60,000 × 50%	(30,000)
	30,000
Depreciation year 2: $30,000 × 50%	(15,000)
	15,000
Depreciation year 3: $7,500 × 50%	(7,500)
	7,500

Non-current asset disposal account

	$		$
Cost (original cost always)	60,000	Accumulated depreciation	52,500
IS (balancing figure)	22,500	Sale proceeds	30,000
	82,500		82,500

23   **C**

Allowance for receivables

	$		$
Bal c/d (10% × 420,000)	42,000	Bal b/d	30,000
		Irrec. debts a/c	12,000
	42,000		42,000

Bad debts expense

	$		$
Allowance for receivables	12,000	Income statement	15,000
Irrec. debts written off	3,000		
	15,000		15,000

Note: Since the irrecoverable debt write off appears in the trial balance, receivables must already have been adjusted.

24   D

25   A

Inventories are valued at lower of cost and net realisable value (costs to be incurred in selling inventories are deducted from selling price in computing NRV)

	Cost	Price less commission	Lower of cost and NRV
A	3,600	4,275	3,600
B	18,600	17,385	17,385
C	2,760	2,651	2,651
			23,636

Here each item A, B and C are looked at separately and not as a group.

26   B

	$
Opening inventories	6,000
Purchases	54,000
Less: Closing inventories	(12,000)
Cost of sales	48,000

		%	$
Sales	Balancing figure	100	64,000
Cost of sales	See above	(75)	(48,000)
Gross profit	25%/75% × $48,000	25	16,000

27   D

	$
Output VAT on sales (20% × $200,000)	40,000
Input VAT on purchases (20/120 × $162,000)	(27,000)
	13,000

28   A

Non-current asset disposal account

Cost	24,000	Accumulated depreciation	21,000
Paid	34,400	New van	36,000
		IS	1,400
	58,400		58,400

12,000 + 6,000 + 3,000 = 21,000

Cost	24,000
Depreciation 50%	(12,000)
	12,000
Depreciation 50%	(6,000)
	6,000
Depreciation 50%	(3,000)

29   A

Rent receivable account

	$		$
Bal b/d (Orsetes)	1,400	Bal b/d (Medea)	1,000
IS (balancing figure)	8,300	Recorded in year (4,000 + 5,000)	9,000
Bal c/d (Orestes)	500	Bal c/d (Medea)	200
	10,200		10,200
Bal b/d (Medea)	200	Bal b/d (Orestes)	500

30 $445,560

445,800 + 7,500 − 6,930 − 1,650 + 840 = 445,560

31   B

14,400 × 9/12 = 10,800 Rent expense

14,400 − 10,800 = 3,600 Prepayment

32   B

$162,000 × 90% = 145,800

The carrying amount of $72,000 of the trade-in old machine is irrelevant. The trade-in value agreed is evidently $45,000, which is the difference between the supplier's price and the cash paid.

33   B

34 $48,400

	$
Purchase of raw material	28,000
Carriage inwards	1,250
Increase in inventories	(850)
Cost of material consumed	28,400
Direct wages	10,500
Prime cost	38,900
Production overheads	7,000
Decrease in work-in-progress	2,500
Production cost	48,400

35   A

The cost of transporting raw materials forms part of the direct material costs.

36   B

Sales	174,000
Opening inventories	14,300
Purchases (see below)	134,800
	149,100
Closing inventories	Balancing figure = $18,273
Cost of sales (see below)	130,827

PLCA

Paid payables	133,650	Bal b/f	3,750
Bal c/d	4,900	Purchases(balancing figure)	134,800
	138,550		138,550

	%		$
Balance	133%	Sales	174,000
Mark-up	100%	(Cost of sales)	???
Given	33%	Gross profit	

Therefore, cost of sales = $174,000 × 100/133 = $130,827

37   D

38   D

39 $244,000

Reconstruction of cost of goods sold to establish the purchases figure:

	$	$
Opening inventories		24,000
Add: Purchases	244,000*	
Less: Returns	(10,000)	234,000
Closing inventories		(36,000)
Cost of goods sold		222,000

Found by difference

40   D

41   False

The main objective of internal audit is to assist the directors of a company in the effective discharge of their financial responsibilities towards the members.

42   D

Electricity			
Cash paid	20,400	Bal b/f	15,000
Bal c/d	17,400	IS	22,800
	37,800		37,800

43   D

A is wrong because the debit to irrecoverable debts would already have been made when the allowance was first set up.

44   A

45   D

46   C

Plant & machinery

	$000		$000
Bal b/f	325	Depreciation	63
		Disposal	12
Additions	200	Bal c/f	450
(bal fig = cash paid)			
	525		525

47   C

Correct entry was to credit purchases returns account with $24,780. To correct, credit purchases returns with $24,780 + $25,860. Suspense account is to be debited, as the original entry will have created a suspense account balance by putting the accounts out of balance.

48   4.9 times

Rate of inventory turnover is found by dividing cost of goods sold by average inventory.

Average inventory = (8,000 + 12,000)/2 = $10,000

Cost of goods sold is $49,000

Rate of inventory turnover is therefore 49,000/10,000 = 4.9 times

49   A

Part of an audit involves determining that the financial statements show a true and fair view, but it does not guarantee that this is the case; in addition, many organisations that do not have an audit performed still produce financial statements that show a true and fair view. Thus answer B is not wholly correct.

50   B

Section 8

ANSWERS TO MOCK ASSESSMENT 2

1   D

2   C

3   D

4   D

The separate entity convention states that the transactions of the business and those of the owner should be kept separate. Therefore, any money, goods or services taken out of the business by the owner should be treated as private transactions.

5   B

54,000 – 18,000 + 36,000 +/– profit/loss = 63,000

Therefore profit/loss = 63,000 – 54,000 + 18,000 – 36,000 = –9,000 (loss)

6   **True**

7   D

8   B

9   **False**

10   B

11   C

12   D

3,204 + 780 – 370 = 3,614

13   C

14   C

15 **$23,920**

	$
Statement balance	26,800
Add back dishonoured cheque	600
Add back bank charges	100
Less: Unpresented cheques	(2,800)
Adjustment re-error	(780) That is twice 390
	23,920

16 **B**

Closing inventories are an asset in the statement of financial position and are deducted from cost of sales (and hence added to profit) in the income statement. An increase of inventories from $25,500 to $27,600 would therefore increase assets and profit by $2,100 = ($27,600 – $25,500).

17 **D**

SLCA

	$		$
Bal b/d	2,000	Cash from credit customers (9,500 – 200)	9,300
Credit sales	13,000	Irrecoverable debt expense (amounts written off only)	200
		Discounts allowed	30
		Return inwards	40
		Bal c/d	5,430
	15,000		15,000

Note that there are a lot of red herrings in the question, for example cash sales, and also entries that are included in PLCA.

18 **A**

Rent and Local business tax expense

	$		$
Bal b/d	60	Bal b/d	300
Cash	2,520	Income statement (bal. fig.)	2,550
Bal c/d	360	Bal c/d	90
	2,940		2,940

19 $76,200

	$
Opening balance	69,000
Credit purchases	156,800
Discounts	(2,400)
Payments	(137,800)
Purchase returns	(9,400)
Closing balance	76,200

PLCA

	$		$
Discounts	2,400	Bal b/f	69,000
Payments	137,800	Credit purchases	156,800
Returns	9,400		
Bal c/d (bal fig)	76,200		
	225,800		225,800

Note cash purchases are not included as they would not be posted to the purchase ledger control account.

20   B

	$
Petty cash float at 1 December	150
Received from staff	15
Cashed cheque	(40)
Cash drawn	300
	425
Petty cash expenses (bal fig)	(245)
Petty cash float at 31 December	180

21   D

A and B would affect both the control account and the ledger in equal amounts. C does not affect the purchase ledger control account, it relates to the sales ledger. The correct answer is D.

22   C

	$
Cost	60,000
Depreciation year 1:10% × $60,000	(6,000)
	54,000
Depreciation year 2:10% × ($60,000 – 6,000)	(5,400)
	48,600

23   A

Van account

	$		$
Bal b/d	18,000	Disposals account	18,000
	18,000		18,000

Accumulated depreciation account

	$		$
Disposals account	13,500	Bal b/d ($18,000 × 25% × 3)	13,500
	13,500		13,500

Disposals account

	$		$
Van (original cost)	18,000	Accumulated depreciation	13,500
Cash	27,600	New van	30,000
		IS (balancing figure)	2,100
	45,600		45,600

24   D

In a receipts and payments account, capital expenditure is charged when it is incurred.

25   C

$330,000 × 2% = $6,600 per year

Accumulated depreciation after 3 years = $6,600 × 3 = $19,800

Carrying value = $468,000 – $19,800 = $448,200

26   A

	$	%
Sales (60,450 + 17,880) – see below for T account	78,330	140
Mark-up		40
Cost of sales (78,330 × 100/140)	55,950	100
Purchases (63,360 + 7,020) – see below for T account	70,380	
Therefore, closing inventories (70,380 – 55,950)	14,430	

Started business hence opening inventories, receivables and payables will be nil.

SLCA

Bal b/f	0	Cash received	60,450
Sales	78,330	Bal c/d	17,880
	78,330		78,330

PLCA

Cash paid	63,360	Bal b/f	0
Bal c/d	7,020	Purchases	70,380
	70,380		70,380

27   A

Rent payable

	$		$
		Accrual b/d	1,500
Rent paid	7,650	Income statement (bal fig)	5,400
		Prepayment c/d (2,250 × 1/3)	750
	7,650		7,650

28   C

Prime cost includes only direct materials and direct production wages.

29   A

($35,800 + $53,400) + $14,800 + $3,600 – $4,700 = $102,900

30   D

31   B

Debentures are debt, not equity.

32   D

Sales tax is not recoverable and therefore must be capitalised as cost of the car.

$198,000 × 20% = $39,600

$198,000 + $39,600 = $237,600

(Cost – residual value)/estimated useful life = (237,600 – 90,000)/3 = $49,200

$237,600 – $49,200 = $188,400

33   D

<table>
<tr><td colspan="4" align="center">**Subscription account (Revenue)**</td></tr>
<tr><td>Accruals b/f</td><td align="right">38</td><td>Prepayment b/f</td><td align="right">72</td></tr>
<tr><td>Income and expenditure
  (Balancing figure)</td><td align="right">792</td><td>Subscription received</td><td align="right">790</td></tr>
<tr><td>Prepaid income</td><td align="right">80</td><td>Accrued income c/d</td><td align="right">48</td></tr>
<tr><td></td><td align="right">910</td><td></td><td align="right">910</td></tr>
</table>

34   A

35   A

36 $720

	Qty	Price $	Total $
Opening inventories	60	4.00	240
Purchases	100	4.80	480
Balance	160	4.50	720
Sales	(80)	4.50	(360)
Balance	80	4.50	360
Purchases	120	5.00	600
Balance	200	4.80	960
Sales	(50)	4.80	(240)
Balance	150		720

37   D

Sales	120,000	160%
Cost of sales	???	100%
Gross profit	???	60%

Therefore:

Cost of sales = 120,000 × 100/160 = 75,000

Gross profit = 120,000 × 60/160 = 45,000

38   C

39   B

Insurance

Bal b/f (prepayment)	1,000		
		I/S charge	5,800
Paid	5,600		
		Bal c/f (bal fig)	800
	6,600		6,600

40 $19,400

	$
Prime cost	112,000
Factory overheads	9,000
Opening work-in-progress	12,400
Factory cost of goods completed	(114,000)
Closing work-in-progress	19,400

41   D

	$
Net wages	320,000
Employees' tax	30,000
Employees' NI	18,000
Gross wages	368,000
Employer's NI	22,000
Cost to company	390,000

42   D

Receivables days = 45 = Receivables (based on average per qn)/sales × 365

Sales = $3,253,680

Therefore average receivables = 45 × $3,253,680/365 = $401,139

$401,139 = (opening receivables of $368,125 + closing receivables)/2

Therefore, closing receivables = ($401,139 × 2) − $368,125 = $434,153

43   **$830,000**

	$000
Operating profit	780
Depreciation	45
Increase in inventories	(13)
Decrease in receivables	23
Decrease in payables	(5)
Cash generated from operations	830

44   **$212,500**

Current ratio = 2.1:1

Current liabilities = $425,000

Therefore current assets = 2.1 × $425,000 = $892,500

Quick (acid test) ratio = 1.6:1

Therefore current assets less inventory = 1.6 × $425,000 = $680,000

Inventory = $892,500 – $680,000 = $212,500

45   **B**

	$000
Issue of share capital	100
Repayment of loans	(200)
Dividends paid	(55)
Net outflow	(155)

46   **D**

47   **C**

48   **A**

49   **False**

50   **B**